Managing iOS Devices with Intune

Intune Playbook Companion Series

Dr. Patrick Jones

OLYMPUS ACADEMY
PRESS

After finishing this book, if you are keen to deepen your knowledge of Intune, you have several options:

- Supplement your learning with other books in the Intune Playbook Companion Series
- Contact Dr. Patrick Jones for information about professional service opportunities
- Check out the online Intune Basics course provided by Olympus Academy, which includes detailed instructions and video tutorials.

Bit.ly/intunebasics

Thank you for supporting this publication and enjoy your learning!

Table of Contents

Introduction to Intune and iOS Management

In today's world, mobile devices have woven themselves into the fabric of our daily work routines. It's hard to imagine a workplace without iPhones or iPads, whether they're being used to check emails, review documents, or join virtual meetings. These devices are not just conveniences; they're tools that increase productivity, enable flexibility, and keep employees connected. But, like any tool, they also need oversight to ensure they're used effectively and securely. That's where mobile device management (MDM) comes into play—and Microsoft Intune is a leading solution.

Managing iOS devices, in particular, is essential for several reasons. First, they are commonly used in corporate environments due to their reliability, security features, and user-friendly design. However, without proper management, these devices can pose security risks. Unsecured devices could lead to data breaches, unauthorized access to sensitive information, and even compliance violations. For organizations of all sizes, ensuring that mobile devices are both productive and secure is a balancing act that requires careful planning and the right tools.

This book focuses on how Intune, a versatile MDM tool from Microsoft, can simplify and strengthen the way your organization manages iOS devices. Intune is part of the Microsoft Endpoint Manager suite, which provides a unified way to manage devices across platforms, including Windows, Android, macOS, and, of course, iOS. But what makes Intune stand out for managing iOS devices, specifically? It's designed to provide both robust security and seamless usability. With Intune, IT administrators can set policies that protect company data while keeping the user experience as intuitive as possible. The goal is to give users the flexibility they need while ensuring that devices remain compliant with corporate policies.

To understand why iOS device management is so crucial, consider the range of tasks employees perform on their devices. Many employees access sensitive emails, log in to business applications, share documents, and store valuable information on their mobile devices. If these devices aren't managed properly, they could become entry points for cyber threats. Mobile devices are inherently portable, which is both a strength and a vulnerability; they can be easily lost, stolen, or accessed by unauthorized individuals. Proper management ensures that if a device falls into the wrong hands, the organization's data remains protected.

Additionally, managing iOS devices helps businesses comply with industry regulations. Many sectors—such as healthcare, finance, and education—have strict standards for data protection. Failing to meet these standards can lead to serious consequences, from financial penalties to reputational damage. Intune enables organizations to enforce compliance policies that align with regulatory requirements, offering peace of mind to both IT teams and company leadership.

A well-managed iOS fleet also contributes to a better user experience. Employees often want to use their own devices for work, a practice known as Bring Your Own Device (BYOD). BYOD programs are popular because they allow employees to work on devices they are comfortable with. But BYOD also requires careful control to keep work data separate from personal data. Intune allows companies to manage both company-owned and BYOD iOS devices, creating a seamless experience for users while protecting corporate information. Employees get the flexibility they want, and IT retains the control it needs.

Microsoft Intune is not just a tool; it's part of a broader vision called Microsoft Endpoint Manager (MEM). Endpoint Manager combines Intune with other management tools, providing a comprehensive solution for managing a wide range of devices in a consistent way. With Endpoint Manager, IT admins can manage everything from laptops and desktops to mobile devices like iPhones and iPads, all from a single platform. This centralization makes it easier to keep track of devices, enforce policies, and monitor compliance across the board.

Intune's strength lies in its flexibility. Whether your organization needs to manage a fleet of corporate-owned iPhones or wants to provide secure access for employees' personal devices, Intune has the features to support both scenarios. For company-owned devices, Intune can enforce stricter security policies and control access to corporate resources. For BYOD devices, Intune offers app-level protections, which means company data can be secured without affecting personal data on the device. This flexibility is key because it allows organizations to adopt the management style that best suits their needs and workforce.

Another advantage of Intune is its integration with the rest of Microsoft 365. Many businesses already use Microsoft 365 for email, file storage, and collaboration, so adding Intune for device management feels like a natural extension. With Intune, admins can manage not only the device but also the applications that users rely on, like Outlook, Teams, and SharePoint. This integrated approach simplifies management and creates a consistent security posture across the organization's entire Microsoft ecosystem.

The modern workplace is defined by mobility and flexibility. Employees are no longer confined to a single location; they work from home, coffee shops, airports, and anywhere else with a Wi-Fi signal. This flexibility has created new challenges for IT departments, which must now manage devices that are not always within the four walls of the office. Intune provides IT teams with the tools to handle these challenges, enabling them to manage devices from the cloud. This cloud-based approach is especially beneficial for organizations with remote or hybrid workforces, as it allows IT to enforce policies and push updates from anywhere, without needing physical access to the device.

In addition, Intune's capabilities extend beyond basic device management. It allows organizations to enforce conditional access policies, which require devices to meet certain standards before they can access company resources. For example, you could require that a device has the latest operating system updates or that it isn't jailbroken before it's allowed access to sensitive data. These conditional access policies create an additional layer of security, ensuring that only compliant devices can connect to the organization's network.

One of the biggest challenges in device management is finding a balance between security and usability. Too many restrictions can frustrate users and hinder productivity, while too few restrictions can leave an organization vulnerable to threats. Intune is designed to strike this balance by providing customizable policies. IT admins can tailor policies to the organization's needs, setting strict security controls for corporate-owned devices and lighter controls for personal devices.

For example, on a corporate-owned iPhone, you might enforce a passcode requirement, restrict access to certain apps, and enable remote wiping if the device is lost. On a BYOD device, you might only require app-level protections, ensuring that company data within apps like Outlook or Teams is secure while leaving the user's personal data untouched. This flexibility helps organizations create a secure environment without sacrificing the user experience.

With Intune, your organization can embrace the benefits of mobile technology without compromising on security or usability. Let's get started on this journey toward mastering iOS device management in a way that's both user-friendly and secure.

Overview of Prerequisites

Before you dive into managing iOS devices with Intune, there are a few foundational elements that need to be set up to ensure a smooth and secure management experience. This section covers the essential prerequisites—licenses, Apple Business Manager, and the MDM push certificate—that form the backbone of your iOS device management strategy in Intune. Having these prerequisites in place will not only make it easier to enroll and manage devices but also enable you to leverage the full range of Intune's features with minimal issues.

1. Microsoft 365 or Intune Licenses

Every organization using Intune needs the appropriate licensing to manage devices effectively. Microsoft Intune is available as part of Microsoft 365 plans, such as Enterprise Mobility + Security (EMS) or Microsoft 365 E3 and E5 subscriptions. The choice of license often depends on your organization's specific needs. For instance, EMS E3 offers core MDM and mobile application management (MAM) capabilities, while EMS E5 includes additional advanced security features.

Each user who will have a managed iOS device needs a license. It's important to assign these licenses to the user accounts in your organization that will be using Intune-managed devices. This ensures that Intune can apply policies, deploy apps, and enforce compliance settings effectively across devices. If you're starting from scratch, make sure you have a clear understanding of which licenses your organization needs, as this will affect both functionality and budget. For many companies, the license structure is flexible enough to adapt as their device management requirements evolve.

2. Apple Business Manager (ABM)

For organizations managing corporate-owned iOS devices, Apple Business Manager (ABM) is essential. ABM is Apple's free portal for organizations to manage device enrollment, purchase apps in bulk, and deploy devices with automated settings. ABM allows you to assign iOS devices to Intune automatically as soon as they're turned on and connected to WiFi, which makes enrollment simple and quick. It's particularly useful for companies that have large numbers of iPhones or iPads to set up and don't want to configure each one manually.

Setting up ABM involves creating an Apple Business Manager account and then linking it to Intune. Once the two systems are connected, devices purchased through Apple or authorized resellers can be assigned to Intune directly within the ABM portal. This allows for zero-touch deployment, meaning users don't need to go through complex setup processes to get started with their devices. Everything from WiFi settings to security policies can be pre-configured, making the initial setup smooth and hassle-free for both users and IT teams.

3. MDM Push Certificate

The Mobile Device Management (MDM) push certificate is another fundamental requirement for managing iOS devices with Intune. This certificate, provided by Apple, allows Intune to communicate with iOS devices over the cloud, enabling the platform to push policies, apps, and settings to devices in real time. Without an active MDM push certificate, Intune cannot manage iOS devices, making this certificate a must-have for any organization using iPhones or iPads within their corporate environment.

Setting up the MDM push certificate involves going through Apple's Push Certificates Portal and generating a certificate that's valid for one year. This certificate needs to be renewed annually, which is critical to keep in mind, as expired certificates can lead to management disruptions. When the certificate expires, Intune loses its ability to communicate with enrolled devices, so setting a reminder for renewal is a best practice.

To generate an MDM push certificate, you'll need an Apple ID, preferably one that's tied to your organization rather than an individual, as it will be used for renewals each year. After generating the certificate in Apple's portal, it's uploaded into Intune, which then enables device enrollment and management capabilities. This process only takes a few minutes, but it's an essential first step that should be done as soon as you're ready to begin iOS device management.

4. Setting Up Intune and Endpoint Manager

While the core requirements focus on licensing, ABM, and the MDM certificate, there are some initial steps within the Intune portal that help create a foundational setup. Within Microsoft Endpoint Manager

(MEM), the portal where Intune lives, admins can set up basic organizational configurations, like branding and enrollment restrictions, to tailor the environment to your organization's specific needs.

Setting up Endpoint Manager for the first time may involve creating an organizational profile, setting up terms of use, and configuring a few basic enrollment settings. You can specify which types of devices are allowed to enroll and restrict OS versions to ensure all enrolled iOS devices meet your company's minimum requirements. These settings are part of establishing a baseline, ensuring that devices meet company standards even before they fully join the management environment.

By configuring these initial settings, you'll also make it easier to implement additional policies down the road, from compliance policies to conditional access settings. Once your Intune environment is configured with the correct setup, managing iOS devices becomes much more streamlined.

A New Path for Alex

Alex stared at the list of new projects in his inbox, his heart thumping a little faster as his eyes landed on one in particular: *"iOS Device Management with Intune - Project Lead: Alex Torres."* He sat back, fingers drumming on his desk as he processed the title. It wasn't that he was unfamiliar with mobile devices—he'd been in IT long enough to know the basics. But managing them on a large scale, specifically iOS devices with Microsoft Intune? That was new territory.

Alex had always prided himself on being up for a challenge. He'd joined the company a few months ago, bringing with him a solid foundation in desktop support and Windows management. But his new manager, Lucy, was the kind of leader who didn't waste any time expanding her team's horizons. When she'd told him last week that she had a "growth opportunity" for him, he hadn't expected this. Managing iOS devices seemed like an advanced task—more fitting for someone with years of experience in mobile device management, not for someone like him, still finding his way in the world of enterprise IT.

Still, Lucy had faith in him, and that meant something. She'd even set him up with a couple of resources to help him get started: a book series called the *Intune Playbook Companion Series* and an online course, *Intune Playbook* from Olympus Academy. Alex had cracked open the first book, flipping through chapters that covered the foundations of Intune and mobile management. He had to admit—it was surprisingly approachable, written in a way that made even complex steps seem straightforward.

His phone buzzed with a message from Lucy: "Ready to dive into iOS management? Start with the basics. Let's chat once you've got a handle on the setup requirements. You've got this!"

The basics. Where did one even start with something as broad as "managing iOS devices"? Alex had heard a few team members talk about the essentials: things like MDM (Mobile Device Management) certificates, licensing, and even something called Apple Business Manager. Each term felt like a puzzle piece, something to connect as he built his understanding. The idea of managing dozens, maybe even hundreds of iPhones and iPads remotely was both exciting and a little overwhelming. He couldn't help but feel a thrill at the idea that he'd be able to deploy settings and apps with the push of a button—or that he could help keep company data safe, no matter where a device was.

As he opened up his laptop to start the Olympus Academy course, Alex was struck by how much IT had changed since he first started. Gone were the days when a company's data was safely stored in an on-premises server. Today, it was all about mobility and remote access. Devices traveled in and out of the office daily, carrying sensitive information with them. Alex realized that his job wasn't just about managing devices—it was about safeguarding his team's work, protecting the company's data from all the unseen risks that came with the territory of remote work.

The course kicked off with an overview of Intune, explaining its role in the larger world of Microsoft Endpoint Manager. He learned about the balancing act: protecting corporate data while ensuring that devices remained easy to use. It was a lot to take in, but he found himself drawn into the process, intrigued by how much there was to learn and how much responsibility he was being given.

By the time he finished the introductory module, Alex had a list of questions. How would he set up the MDM push certificate? Did he need a special Apple account for that Apple Business Manager thing? And how would he make sure users didn't feel like their devices were being taken over by IT? As the questions filled his mind, he knew he was only scratching the surface, but he was already looking forward to uncovering more. He could feel himself growing into the role, bit by bit.

As he shut down his laptop for the evening, a smile crept onto his face. The task ahead felt enormous, but also like exactly the kind of challenge he'd been hoping for. The journey had just begun, and he couldn't wait to see where it would lead.

Will Alex find his footing as he tackles the foundational requirements of iOS management in Intune? Stay tuned as he delves into the nuts and bolts of setup, facing new puzzles and uncovering the secrets of mobile device management in the chapters to come.

Summary and Reflection

In this chapter, we introduced the essentials of managing iOS devices using Microsoft Intune. We explored why iOS device management is crucial in today's mobile workplace, with devices carrying sensitive data outside of traditional office environments. We discussed the role of Intune within Microsoft Endpoint Manager, which provides a unified platform for managing both mobile devices and traditional workstations. This structure gives IT teams the flexibility to secure data and applications while supporting a mobile, modern workforce.

We also reviewed the basic setup requirements for Intune, including Microsoft 365 or Intune licenses, Apple Business Manager (ABM) for corporate-owned device enrollment, and the MDM push certificate. These prerequisites form the technical foundation needed to enable Intune's communication with Apple devices, providing IT teams with the tools to enforce security policies and manage devices effectively. Establishing this solid foundation allows organizations to manage devices confidently, knowing they have the necessary resources to maintain security and compliance.

In this chapter, we followed Alex as he took his first steps into the world of iOS device management with Intune. For Alex, the process of understanding Intune's role in device management and setting up these foundational elements wasn't just about learning new terms—it was an initiation into the broader responsibilities of modern IT management. Like many IT professionals, Alex quickly saw that managing devices isn't only about applying security policies; it's about supporting the mobile nature of today's workplace while ensuring users feel confident and comfortable with the tools provided.

As you reflect on your journey so far, consider how Alex's experiences parallel your own. Setting up the prerequisites for Intune might feel technical, but it also marks the start of creating a supportive environment for users. Just as Alex began by understanding why these foundational pieces matter, you too are establishing a base that allows you to effectively manage, secure, and support iOS devices across your organization. Each of these setup steps—connecting Apple Business Manager, generating an MDM push certificate, and ensuring licenses are in place—will make all future device management tasks more streamlined and secure.

Alex's attention to detail in the setup phase reflects an important lesson for anyone entering iOS device management: success begins with careful planning and configuration. By building a solid foundation now, you're not only preparing for immediate device needs but also setting up a system that can grow and adapt as your organization's mobile needs evolve. This foundation empowers you to approach the next steps with confidence, knowing you've built a secure, reliable environment for iOS device management.

With the initial setup complete, you're ready to dive into the next stage of Intune management—configuring Intune for optimal iOS device management. Just as Alex is prepared to connect the technical elements of Intune to real-world applications, you'll learn how to configure Apple enrollment programs, create MDM push certificates, and assign enrollment profiles to provide a smooth experience for users.

Alex's journey continues, and so does yours, as you begin building out Intune's capabilities to create a fully configured, efficient, and secure environment for iOS device management.

Configuring Intune for iOS Devices

For organizations managing corporate-owned iOS devices, connecting Apple Business Manager (ABM) to Intune is a foundational step. Apple Business Manager is Apple's portal designed to streamline device deployment and management for businesses. By linking ABM with Intune, IT admins can create a seamless, automated enrollment experience for iOS devices, enabling users to receive pre-configured settings and applications the moment they power up their devices. This setup not only saves time but also provides the control necessary to ensure devices meet organizational security standards from day one.

Let's walk through the setup process step-by-step, from understanding what ABM offers to configuring the connection between ABM and Intune.

Apple Business Manager is a free service from Apple that helps organizations manage large fleets of iOS devices. Through ABM, IT admins can automate the initial device setup, pre-assign devices to specific management tools (like Intune), and purchase apps in bulk. With ABM, devices bought directly from Apple or authorized resellers can be enrolled in Intune right out of the box—no manual setup needed. This zero-touch deployment means that devices are configured and ready for use as soon as the user powers them on and connects to WiFi.

In addition to streamlining enrollment, ABM allows organizations to:

- **Define Enrollment Profiles**: Specify device settings, like WiFi networks or specific security configurations, before devices are even unboxed.

- **Enforce Security Policies**: Ensure that corporate-owned devices have the right security settings from the start.

- **Purchase Apps in Bulk**: Buy licenses for apps and distribute them through Intune, ensuring employees have access to the tools they need.

By integrating ABM with Intune, organizations can bring these benefits to life, making device deployment efficient and secure.

Steps to Connect Apple Business Manager to Intune

Setting up Apple Business Manager to work with Intune involves a few essential steps. While the process is straightforward, each step is crucial for ensuring that devices are enrolled correctly and that Intune can push policies, settings, and apps to each iOS device.

Step 1: Prepare an Apple ID for ABM

To connect ABM with Intune, you'll need an Apple ID tied to your organization, ideally a generic account managed by the IT department. Avoid using personal Apple IDs or IDs tied to individuals, as this account will need to be accessed periodically for updates and renewals.

If your organization doesn't already have an Apple Business Manager account, you can register one on Apple's website. The process is straightforward, though it may take a couple of days for Apple to verify your organization.

Step 2: Generate a Server Token in Apple Business Manager

Once you're logged into ABM, it's time to create a server token. The server token is what links ABM to Intune, allowing the two systems to communicate and ensuring that devices purchased through Apple or resellers are automatically enrolled in Intune.

1. Log in to Apple Business Manager with your organization's Apple ID.
2. Navigate to Settings and select Device Management Settings.

3. Click Add MDM Server and give the server a name (e.g., "Intune").

4. Once the server is created, download the server token. This token file will be uploaded to Intune in the next steps, establishing the connection between ABM and Intune.

This token is valid for one year, so make a note to renew it annually to avoid any disruptions in device management.

Step 3: Upload the Server Token to Intune

With the server token in hand, the next step is to upload it to Intune to establish the link.

1. Open the Microsoft Endpoint Manager admin center and navigate to Devices > iOS/iPadOS > iOS Enrollment.

2. Select Apple Enrollment and click on Apple MDM Push Certificate.

3. In the options that appear, locate the Apple Business Manager Server Token section.

4. Click Upload Token and select the server token file you downloaded from ABM.

5. Intune will validate the token and confirm that the connection between ABM and Intune has been established.

This connection allows Intune to recognize devices assigned to it within ABM and to manage them according to the enrollment profiles you set.

Step 4: Assign Devices to Intune in ABM

With the connection established, the next task is to assign devices to the Intune MDM server within Apple Business Manager. This step ensures that new devices purchased through Apple or resellers will be automatically enrolled in Intune when powered on.

1. In Apple Business Manager, go to Devices.

2. Select the devices you want to assign to Intune (you can filter devices by purchase order, serial number, or model).

3. Under Manage MDM Servers, assign the selected devices to the Intune server you created earlier.

Once devices are assigned to Intune in ABM, they are now ready for automatic enrollment. The next time a user turns on the device and connects to WiFi, the device will automatically connect to Intune and apply the settings and policies configured for it.

Step 5: Create Enrollment Profiles in Intune

After assigning devices to Intune in ABM, the final step is to set up enrollment profiles in Intune. Enrollment profiles specify the settings that will be applied to devices when they first enroll, such as WiFi configurations, app deployments, and security policies.

1. In Microsoft Endpoint Manager, navigate to Devices > iOS/iPadOS > iOS Enrollment.

2. Select Enrollment Program Tokens and choose the token associated with your ABM connection.

3. Click Create Profile to create an enrollment profile. In this profile, define the settings you want applied to new devices during enrollment, such as enabling Multi-Factor Authentication (MFA), setting passcode requirements, or configuring WiFi networks.

Enrollment profiles make it easy to automate device configuration, ensuring that devices meet your organization's standards from the moment they connect to the network. By the time the user completes setup, the device is ready to go, with all necessary apps, security policies, and configurations in place.

Connecting ABM to Intune simplifies the deployment of iOS devices and adds an extra layer of security. The benefits of automatic enrollment go beyond time savings; they ensure that every device is compliant with company standards from the moment it's turned on. This automation is especially valuable for organizations with distributed teams or employees working remotely, as it eliminates the need for IT to configure each device manually.

Creating MDM Push Certificates: Step-by-Step Guide

The MDM (Mobile Device Management) push certificate is a critical component of iOS device management within Intune. This certificate, provided by Apple, acts as a secure communication bridge between Intune and your organization's iOS devices, allowing Intune to push settings, apps, and policies to devices remotely. Without a valid MDM push certificate, Intune cannot enroll or manage iOS devices. Setting up this certificate is essential for maintaining seamless management capabilities, and renewing it on time is crucial to avoid interruptions.

Here's a straightforward, step-by-step guide on how to set up the MDM push certificate for your organization's Intune environment.

Step 1: Prepare Your Apple ID

Before you can create the MDM push certificate, you'll need an Apple ID. To keep things organized and secure, it's best to use an Apple ID specifically created for your organization, rather than a personal Apple ID or one tied to an individual. This Apple ID will be used annually to renew the certificate, so it's helpful to have a shared account that your IT team can access if needed. Make a note of this Apple ID, as you'll need it each time the certificate is renewed.

Step 2: Sign into the Microsoft Endpoint Manager Admin Center

1. Open a web browser and go to the Microsoft Endpoint Manager Admin Center.

2. Sign in using your organization's administrator credentials.

3. In the Endpoint Manager dashboard, navigate to Devices > iOS/iPadOS > iOS Enrollment.

This section of the portal is where all iOS enrollment settings are managed. Here, you'll find options for configuring Apple Business Manager integration, enrollment profiles, and the MDM push certificate.

Step 3: Initiate the MDM Push Certificate Setup

Once you're in the iOS Enrollment section, it's time to initiate the process of setting up the MDM push certificate.

1. Select Apple MDM Push Certificate from the available options.

2. You'll see a prompt explaining the purpose of the certificate and providing a link to Apple's Push Certificates Portal. Click on Download your CSR (Certificate Signing Request) file. This file is used to request the MDM push certificate from Apple.

Downloading the CSR file is a crucial step, as it contains information that Apple uses to verify the request. Keep the CSR file handy, as you'll need it in the next step.

Step 4: Access the Apple Push Certificates Portal

Now that you have the CSR file, it's time to visit the Apple Push Certificates Portal to create the actual MDM push certificate.

1. Open a new browser tab and navigate to the Apple Push Certificates Portal.

2. Sign in using the Apple ID you prepared earlier.

3. Once logged in, click Create a Certificate to begin the setup process.

This portal is the location where Apple allows organizations to create and manage MDM certificates for device management. Make sure to keep your login information secure, as you'll return here annually to renew the certificate.

Step 5: Upload the CSR File and Generate the Certificate

With your CSR file ready and your Apple ID logged in, you're now set to create the MDM push certificate.

1. In the Apple Push Certificates Portal, select Choose File and upload the CSR file you downloaded from the Microsoft Endpoint Manager Admin Center.

2. After uploading, click Upload to proceed.

3. Apple will generate the MDM push certificate based on the information in the CSR file. Once the certificate is created, you'll see a prompt to download it. Click Download and save the certificate (.pem file) to your computer.

This certificate (.pem file) is the key that allows Intune to securely communicate with your iOS devices. It will be valid for one year, so be sure to set a calendar reminder for renewal to avoid any service disruptions.

Step 6: Upload the MDM Push Certificate to Intune

The final step is to upload the newly created MDM push certificate into Intune. This connects the certificate with your Intune environment, allowing Intune to manage iOS devices.

1. Return to the Microsoft Endpoint Manager Admin Center and ensure you're still in the Apple MDM Push Certificate section.

2. Click Upload Certificate and select the .pem file you downloaded from the Apple Push Certificates Portal.

3. After uploading, click Save to complete the setup.

Once the certificate is uploaded, Intune will validate the certificate and establish a secure connection to Apple's servers. This connection is what allows Intune to manage iOS devices in your organization, pushing settings, apps, and policies as needed.

Step 7: Verify the Certificate Status

To confirm that the certificate has been uploaded successfully, check the status of the MDM push certificate in the **iOS Enrollment** section of the Endpoint Manager. The certificate should display as "Active," along with the Apple ID used to create it and the expiration date.

Regularly verifying the certificate's status is a best practice, especially as it nears expiration. If the certificate expires, Intune will lose its ability to manage iOS devices until it is renewed. Fortunately, the renewal process is similar to the initial setup, and keeping the same Apple ID streamlines the process.

The MDM push certificate is the linchpin of iOS device management with Intune. Without this certificate, Intune can't communicate with Apple's services, which means it can't manage or enforce any policies on iOS devices. This certificate allows Intune to send commands, deploy apps, and push updates to your organization's devices remotely. In short, it's the foundation of secure, effective iOS management in Intune.

Setting up the MDM push certificate might seem like a minor step, but it's one of the most important parts of configuring Intune for iOS device management. Once it's set up, your organization is ready to start enrolling iOS devices and enforcing the policies that keep company data secure.

Assigning Enrollment Profiles: Simplifying the Process for Users

Once Apple Business Manager (ABM) and the MDM push certificate are set up, the next essential step is to create and assign enrollment profiles for your iOS devices. Enrollment profiles define the initial setup configurations applied to each device during enrollment. These profiles are critical in delivering a seamless, efficient onboarding experience for users by automatically configuring devices to align with your organization's policies and requirements. From enabling WiFi connectivity to enforcing security settings, enrollment profiles simplify the process for users while giving IT teams the control they need.

An enrollment profile is essentially a blueprint that Intune uses to apply settings to devices as they're enrolled. These profiles can specify various settings, including user authentication requirements, Multi-Factor Authentication (MFA) options, and even company branding to provide a tailored experience. By pre-configuring these settings, IT teams can reduce the manual configuration steps required from users, making the device setup as straightforward as possible.

With enrollment profiles, IT can establish a consistent baseline across all devices. This consistency is key for maintaining security and compliance, as it ensures that each device meets organizational standards from the moment it connects to the network.

Types of Enrollment Profiles in Intune

Intune offers a couple of profile options for enrolling iOS devices:

1. **Corporate-Owned Enrollment**: For devices purchased and provided by the organization, this enrollment profile ensures full control over the device, allowing IT to apply comprehensive policies and configurations.

2. **User-Enrolled (BYOD) Enrollment**: For personally-owned devices, this type of profile applies lighter management to

maintain a balance between security and user privacy. Here, Intune applies only app protection policies, allowing users to access work apps without impacting their personal data.

3. **Device Enrollment Program (DEP) Profile**: This profile, created through the connection with Apple Business Manager, enables zero-touch enrollment for corporate-owned devices, providing an effortless setup experience for users.

In this guide, we'll focus on DEP profiles, as they're ideal for streamlining the enrollment of corporate-owned devices purchased through Apple Business Manager.

Step-by-Step Guide to Creating an Enrollment Profile

Let's walk through the process of creating an enrollment profile for iOS devices in Intune:

Step 1: Access the iOS Enrollment Profiles in Intune

1. Go to the Microsoft Endpoint Manager Admin Center and sign in with your administrator credentials.

2. From the main dashboard, navigate to Devices > iOS/iPadOS > iOS Enrollment.

3. Under iOS Enrollment, select Enrollment Program Tokens and then choose the token associated with your Apple Business Manager (ABM) setup.

This brings you to the section where you can manage and create profiles associated with ABM.

Step 2: Create a New Enrollment Profile

1. Select Create Profile to start setting up a new DEP enrollment profile.

2. Enter a name and an optional description for the profile. For example, "Corporate iOS Enrollment" or "Sales Team Devices."

3. Choose the authentication method that suits your organization's needs:

   o **Setup Assistant with Modern Authentication**: Ideal if you want users to sign in using their company credentials during setup.

   o **Automated Device Enrollment**: Automatically configures the device with settings without requiring user authentication, useful for shared or kiosk devices.

Step 3: Configure Profile Settings

Now, you'll configure the specific settings for the enrollment profile:

- **Language and Region**: Set a default language and region to save users from selecting these manually during setup.

- **Skip Setup Assistant Steps**: This option lets you choose which steps in the iOS Setup Assistant are skipped to streamline onboarding. For instance, you can skip steps like Location Services, Apple ID, and Siri setup to speed up the process.

- **Device Supervision**: Enabling supervision grants IT more control over the device, including additional security policies. Supervised mode is ideal for corporate-owned devices, as it allows for remote management capabilities.

- **Shared iPad Configuration** (optional): If your organization uses shared iPads, enabling this setting lets multiple users sign in to the same device with separate profiles, a feature commonly used in education and retail environments.

The profile settings you choose here are applied automatically when devices are powered on and connected to WiFi, making the initial setup quicker and simpler for users.

Step 4: Assign Enrollment Profile to Devices in ABM

Once the enrollment profile is created in Intune, the next step is to assign it to devices in Apple Business Manager. This assignment links the profile to the specific devices purchased through ABM, ensuring they're automatically enrolled with the correct settings when turned on.

1. Open Apple Business Manager and go to Devices.

2. Select the devices you want to assign to the new profile, either individually or by using filters based on purchase order, model, or serial number.

3. Under Manage MDM Servers, select the Intune MDM server you configured and assign the newly created enrollment profile to these devices.

This setup ensures that when users power on their devices, they'll be automatically enrolled in Intune with the designated configurations.

Step 5: Customize Enrollment Notifications and Branding (Optional)

To make the enrollment process more user-friendly, consider adding custom branding and enrollment notifications in Intune. This can include your company's logo, custom terms of use, and a welcome message. Custom branding makes the setup process feel more professional and familiar, helping users feel connected to the organization from the start.

1. In the Microsoft Endpoint Manager Admin Center, go to Tenant Administration > Customization.

2. Add company logos, sign-in messages, and terms of use.

3. Save these settings, which will then appear on user screens during the enrollment process.

Customizing the enrollment experience reinforces trust and familiarity, especially for new hires or team members receiving devices for the first time.

Enrollment profiles are designed to save time and reduce confusion for users. By pre-configuring essential settings, IT admins can streamline the onboarding experience, minimizing the need for users to manually set up their devices. Here are some key benefits of using enrollment profiles:

- **Time Efficiency**: Devices are ready for use immediately after enrollment, with all necessary configurations already in place.

- **Enhanced Security**: Policies such as passcode requirements, encryption, and supervised mode ensure that devices are secure from the start.

- **User Satisfaction**: By simplifying the setup process, enrollment profiles create a smoother experience for users, reducing support requests and enhancing productivity.

Once enrollment profiles are set up, it's important to review and update them periodically. As organizational needs evolve, certain settings may need adjustment to remain relevant and effective. Updating profiles ensures that future device enrollments continue to meet the latest security standards and user expectations.

To edit an existing profile:

1. In the Microsoft Endpoint Manager Admin Center, navigate to Devices > iOS/iPadOS > iOS Enrollment.

2. Select Enrollment Program Tokens and open the profile you want to edit.

3. Make your adjustments, save changes, and reassign the profile to any new devices.

Enrollment profiles are a cornerstone of iOS device management with Intune, allowing IT teams to create a consistent, secure, and user-friendly setup experience. By setting up profiles tailored to specific roles or departments, organizations can standardize configurations, ensuring that each device meets company requirements while minimizing user involvement in the initial setup.

Configuring for Success

Alex leaned back in his chair, taking a deep breath. Today was the day he'd tackle the next step in his iOS device management journey: setting up the backbone for Apple device enrollment and getting his Intune environment ready to handle iPhones and iPads. He felt that familiar thrill of learning something new but was also acutely aware of the challenges ahead. Managing devices was one thing, but setting up Intune to communicate seamlessly with Apple systems? That was a whole new world.

He opened up his copy of the *Intune Playbook Companion Series*. The next chapter was all about setting up Apple Business Manager (ABM) and MDM Push Certificates. Just reading the terms made Alex feel like he was jumping into the deep end. But he was ready to dive in.

His first task: connecting Apple Business Manager (ABM) to Intune. The book explained how ABM could automate the enrollment process for Apple devices, allowing users to power on their iPhones or iPads and have everything pre-configured and ready to go. For Alex, the idea of "zero-touch deployment" sounded like magic. The fewer manual steps there were, the fewer chances for something to go wrong. He read through the steps in the book, noting the need for an organizational Apple ID. It seemed straightforward, but he quickly realized he'd need to collaborate with his team to get the right account set up. He reached out to Lucy for confirmation on the shared Apple ID they'd use, noting down each step he'd need to follow once he had the credentials.

After setting up the account, the directions moved on to the MDM Push Certificate—the piece that would let Intune send commands directly to iOS devices. Without it, Intune wouldn't be able to manage any of the Apple devices on the network. Alex downloaded the Certificate Signing Request (CSR) file, following along as the book guided him through the steps to upload it to Apple's portal. Logging in with their organizational Apple ID, he uploaded the CSR, downloaded the certificate, and returned to Intune to complete the connection.

As he uploaded the certificate file to Intune, a message confirmed that Intune could now securely manage Apple devices. Alex leaned back with a small smile of accomplishment. He knew that something as small as a certificate could be easy to overlook, but it was this piece that ensured everything worked seamlessly. "Not bad," he muttered, feeling the satisfaction of getting it right on his first try.

With ABM and the MDM push certificate set up, it was time to create an enrollment profile. The idea was that these profiles would configure each device the moment it powered on, automatically applying the right settings for company use. This wasn't just about making things easier for users—though he could already see how helpful that would be. It was also about security, ensuring that every device had a consistent baseline of settings, no matter where it was being used.

As Alex started configuring the profile, he saw options that let him tailor the setup: language preferences, whether certain setup screens could be skipped, and the level of security applied to each device. He selected the profile options carefully, aiming for a setup that would make users feel welcomed and reduce the need for support calls. He especially liked the option to skip the Apple ID setup screen. This way, users wouldn't need to sign in with their personal accounts on company-owned devices—a small detail that Alex knew would make a big difference.

The idea of device supervision was another powerful option he encountered. By enabling supervision, the company could control even more aspects of each iOS device, such as preventing users from installing certain apps or restricting access to specific device features. It felt like a lot of control, and Alex thought about it carefully. He imagined how supervised devices would be ideal for field staff who needed strict access controls or for devices used in shared spaces. He decided to enable it for corporate-owned devices, feeling confident in the enhanced security it would bring.

With his enrollment profile complete, he sat back, admiring the final product. The next step would be to test it out—though that would require some coordination with Lucy and the team to get a test device. But as he looked over the profile settings, he was hit by a wave of satisfaction. He had started the day feeling daunted by all the new terms and processes, but now he had built a profile that would make life easier for users and safer for the company.

As Alex packed up for the day, he couldn't help but smile, thinking about the journey so far. The foundational pieces were in place. He had tackled the basics, configured ABM and the MDM certificate, and created a customized enrollment profile. Each step felt like a building block, creating a solid foundation for what would come next.

Would Alex's new configurations hold up when it came time to test? Stay tuned as he explores Intune's powerful policies, discovering the next steps to protect devices and data effectively.

Summary and Reflection

In this chapter, we covered the foundational steps for configuring Intune to manage iOS devices effectively, including connecting Apple Business Manager (ABM) to Intune, creating the MDM push certificate, and assigning enrollment profiles. Each of these setup processes is essential for establishing a secure and seamless device management environment that will serve as the backbone for managing iOS devices within your organization.

We began by exploring how Apple Business Manager (ABM) enables automated enrollment for corporate-owned devices, ensuring that devices are ready for use as soon as they're powered on and connected to WiFi. Then, we walked through the steps of creating the MDM push certificate, which is crucial for enabling secure communication between Intune and iOS devices. Finally, we discussed assigning enrollment profiles to pre-configure devices with the necessary settings, policies, and apps, making the enrollment experience as smooth as possible for users.

These setup steps ensure that devices meet organizational security standards from the start, streamlining deployment and reducing the need for manual configuration. By building a solid foundation, IT teams can simplify device management while enhancing security, compliance, and user experience.

We also followed Alex as he tackled the configuration of Intune for iOS devices, navigating each step with a mix of curiosity and determination. For Alex, connecting ABM, creating the MDM push certificate, and setting up enrollment profiles weren't just technical tasks—they were building blocks in understanding how Intune's infrastructure works and why each element is vital for successful device management. He learned that setting up Intune is more than following steps; it's about creating a streamlined process that makes the user experience effortless and aligns with company security goals.

As you reflect on your own learning journey, consider how Alex's approach mirrors your path. Just as he worked through each configuration step methodically, you are setting up the framework that will support all future device management activities. Building this foundation allows you to feel confident that your iOS devices are secure, compliant, and ready for the next stages of management.

Alex's attention to detail, especially in assigning custom enrollment profiles, reflects a lesson that IT professionals know well: small adjustments make a big difference in user experience and security. By focusing on simplifying the setup process and ensuring devices are configured according to organizational standards, you're not only making your job easier but also building trust with users. A well-prepared configuration makes it clear to users that IT has considered their needs and optimized the system to work for them, not against them.

With the configuration complete, the next step is enrolling iOS devices into Intune. Just as Alex is preparing to guide users through the enrollment process, you're now ready to learn how to set up devices smoothly, whether they're corporate-owned or part of a BYOD program.

Alex's journey continues, as does yours, into the practical aspects of managing devices day-to-day. By mastering enrollment, you'll ensure that users feel supported and empowered while helping your organization maintain a high standard of security.

Enrolling iOS Devices

Options for Enrollment

Enrolling iOS devices into Intune marks a significant step in establishing consistent security, compliance, and user productivity across your organization's mobile devices. Enrollment connects each device to Intune, allowing IT to apply policies, push apps, and secure corporate data. Intune offers several enrollment options to accommodate different types of users, devices, and ownership models, with two primary methods: user-initiated enrollment and automatic enrollment. Each method serves distinct scenarios, offering flexibility in managing devices based on your organization's unique needs.

User-Initiated Enrollment

User-initiated enrollment is a flexible option often used for Bring Your Own Device (BYOD) scenarios, where employees bring their personal devices to work and need access to corporate apps and resources. This method allows users to initiate the enrollment process themselves, with guidance from IT as needed. With user-initiated enrollment, users download the Company Portal app on their devices, sign in with their corporate credentials, and follow a step-by-step setup to connect to Intune.

This enrollment method is ideal for organizations that allow employees to use personal devices for work tasks, as it respects the boundary between work and personal data. With user-initiated enrollment, IT can enforce app-level security for specific work-related apps without having to manage the entire device. Here's how it works:

1. **Download the Company Portal App**: Users download the Company Portal app from the App Store, which serves as the gateway to Intune for their device.

2. **Sign in with Work Credentials**: Once the app is installed, users open it and sign in using their organizational email and password.

3. **Complete the Enrollment Process**: The Company Portal app guides users through a series of prompts to complete the enrollment. This includes accepting terms of use, enabling device management permissions, and configuring any required security settings, like a passcode.

User-initiated enrollment is particularly user-friendly, as it provides clear instructions, step-by-step guidance, and privacy options that keep personal data separate from corporate data. This approach is commonly used for:

- **BYOD Devices**: Employees' personal iPhones or iPads that need limited access to work apps and data.

- **Contractor or Temporary Devices**: Devices that need only short-term access to corporate resources.

- **Light Management Scenarios**: Situations where IT wants to control app access and data security without managing the entire device.

Since user-initiated enrollment focuses on app protection rather than full device control, it allows users to feel more comfortable enrolling personal devices without concerns about their privacy being compromised.

Automatic Enrollment

Automatic enrollment, on the other hand, is designed for corporate-owned devices and provides a more comprehensive level of management and security. Through this method, devices are automatically enrolled in Intune without requiring manual steps from users. Automatic enrollment typically uses Apple Business Manager (ABM) in conjunction with Intune, enabling zero-touch deployment for iOS devices purchased directly through Apple or authorized resellers. This method makes it easy for organizations to pre-configure devices, so they're ready for use right out of the box.

With automatic enrollment, users can power on their devices, connect to WiFi, and instantly receive all necessary settings, apps, and security policies. The device enrolls into Intune without any manual intervention from the user, which makes it a perfect choice for large-scale deployments and distributed workforces. Here's how automatic enrollment works:

1. **Purchase Devices Through ABM**: Corporate-owned iOS devices must be purchased through Apple Business Manager or authorized resellers to support automatic enrollment.

2. **Assign Devices to Intune in ABM**: In Apple Business Manager, IT assigns the purchased devices to Intune, linking them to the organization's MDM server. This ensures that any new devices assigned to the Intune MDM server will automatically enroll when powered on.

3. **Pre-Configure Enrollment Profiles**: IT creates enrollment profiles in Intune, specifying the settings, apps, and security policies each device should receive.

4. **Device Powers On and Connects to WiFi**: When the user powers on the device for the first time and connects to WiFi, it automatically enrolls in Intune, downloading all pre-configured settings and apps.

Automatic enrollment is ideal for scenarios where IT needs more control over devices and can be particularly beneficial in the following cases:

- **Corporate-Owned Devices**: Devices that are the property of the organization and used strictly for work purposes.

- **High-Security Environments**: Industries like healthcare or finance, where devices must meet strict security standards.

- **Distributed Workforce**: Teams working in different locations who require standardized setups without needing on-site IT support.

- **Zero-Touch Deployment**: Situations where devices should be set up and ready for use with minimal user interaction, allowing for a seamless onboarding experience.

Automatic enrollment enables IT to maintain a high level of consistency across devices, ensuring they're equipped with necessary policies, security settings, and applications. It also reduces the risk of misconfiguration and human error, as the process is fully automated from start to finish.

When deciding between user-initiated and automatic enrollment, it's essential to consider your organization's device management policies, security requirements, and user preferences. Here's a quick comparison of when to use each method:

- **User-Initiated Enrollment**:
  - Best for BYOD or personal devices.
  - Limited to app-level management and specific work-related apps.
  - Suitable for contractors, freelancers, and short-term access needs.
  - Balances security with user privacy, keeping personal and work data separate.

- **Automatic Enrollment**:
  - Ideal for corporate-owned devices requiring comprehensive management.
  - Suitable for high-security environments needing standardized device setups.
  - Provides a zero-touch deployment experience, minimizing manual steps for users.

      o   Enforces full device management, enabling detailed security policies and configurations.

Organizations often use both methods, with user-initiated enrollment for BYOD policies and automatic enrollment for corporate-owned devices. The flexibility to choose based on the device ownership model allows IT teams to meet the unique needs of each group within the organization.

Regardless of the enrollment method, seamless enrollment benefits both users and IT teams. For users, an efficient enrollment process reduces the time spent on initial setup, allowing them to get to work faster and with minimal hassle. For IT, consistent and secure enrollment improves device compliance, supports efficient policy management, and enhances security.

Selecting the right enrollment method also builds trust within the organization. Employees feel more comfortable using their devices when they know that their personal data remains private, and IT has peace of mind knowing that corporate data is secure.

BYOD vs. Corporate-Owned Devices

One of the key advantages of Microsoft Intune is its flexibility in managing a variety of device ownership models, including Bring Your Own Device (BYOD) and corporate-owned devices. Each type of device comes with unique needs and challenges, especially regarding privacy, control, and security. Intune allows IT teams to apply different policies and management settings based on the ownership type, ensuring that both user privacy and organizational security requirements are met.

Understanding BYOD (Bring Your Own Device)

BYOD, or Bring Your Own Device, refers to devices that employees own personally but use for work-related tasks. BYOD programs allow employees to use their preferred devices, which often improves productivity and job satisfaction. However, BYOD presents challenges for IT, as personal devices require a balanced approach that protects corporate data while respecting user privacy.

For BYOD devices, Intune focuses on App Protection Policies (APP) and Mobile Application Management (MAM) rather than full device management. This means IT can secure corporate apps and data on the device without intruding into the user's personal files, photos, and other data. With BYOD, Intune applies policies only to work-related apps, such as Outlook, Teams, and OneDrive, while keeping personal data separate. Here's how Intune manages BYOD devices:

1. **App Protection Policies (APP)**: Intune uses app-level policies to protect corporate data within specific apps. For example, IT can enforce data encryption, prevent data sharing between work and personal apps, and require passcodes to access work apps. These protections ensure that corporate information remains secure even on personal devices.

2. **Conditional Access**: Conditional access policies restrict app access to only compliant devices. For instance, users may need to have the latest OS updates or enable specific security settings on their device to access company resources.

3. **Selective Wipe**: If a user leaves the organization or no longer requires access to work apps, Intune can perform a selective wipe. This action removes all corporate data and apps from the device while leaving personal data untouched, ensuring data security without compromising user privacy.

BYOD policies are designed to minimize invasiveness, protecting work data within specified apps without impacting personal data. This balance allows employees to use their devices freely while providing the organization with essential security controls.

Corporate-Owned Devices

Corporate-owned devices, on the other hand, belong to the organization and are often provided to employees specifically for work purposes. Since these devices are company property, IT departments typically apply more comprehensive management and security policies. Unlike BYOD, corporate-owned devices are usually managed at the device level rather than the app level, allowing for greater control over the entire device.

For corporate-owned devices, Intune offers full Mobile Device Management (MDM) capabilities, enabling IT to configure, monitor, and secure the entire device. Here's how Intune manages corporate-owned devices differently from BYOD devices:

1. **Device Compliance Policies**: IT can enforce device-level compliance policies, such as passcode requirements, encryption, and minimum OS versions, to ensure devices meet organizational security standards.

2. **Device Configuration Profiles**: With corporate-owned devices, IT can apply configuration profiles that control WiFi settings, VPN access, email setup, and other device-wide configurations. This allows IT to provide a seamless user experience with pre-configured settings.

3. **Full Remote Management**: Intune enables IT to remotely control corporate-owned devices, offering options such as locking, resetting, or wiping devices if they are lost, stolen, or compromised.

4. **Supervision Mode**: For iOS devices, enabling supervision mode provides additional control over device functionality, such as restricting specific apps, limiting settings, and enforcing strict security policies. Supervised mode is particularly useful in high-security environments, allowing IT to disable features like AirDrop or access to Apple's App Store.

With corporate-owned devices, IT has the flexibility to enforce stricter policies, as users expect these devices to be used primarily for work. By leveraging device-wide controls, Intune ensures that corporate-owned devices are fully compliant, secure, and optimized for productivity.

Comparison: BYOD vs. Corporate-Owned Device Management

When it comes to managing BYOD and corporate-owned devices, Intune's approach differs significantly. Here's a quick comparison of how Intune handles each type of device:

Feature	BYOD Devices	Corporate-Owned Devices
Policy Focus	App-level security (APP, MAM)	Device-level security (MDM)
Control Level	Limited control over apps only	Full device control, including OS settings
Data Privacy	High; no access to personal data	Lower; IT manages entire device
Data Wipe	Selective wipe of work apps/data only	Full device wipe, if necessary
Enrollment Method	User-initiated enrollment	Automatic or ABM-managed enrollment
Device Configuration	App configurations only	WiFi, VPN, email, and device settings
Supervision Mode	Not applicable	Available; adds further control

Best Practices for Managing BYOD and Corporate-Owned Devices

Managing a mix of BYOD and corporate-owned devices can be challenging, especially when trying to balance security and user experience. Here are some best practices to consider:

1. **Define Clear Policies for Each Device Type**: Establish policies that specify the level of management, security requirements, and acceptable use for BYOD vs. corporate-owned devices. This transparency builds trust and reduces confusion for end users.

2. **Use Conditional Access for Consistency**: Conditional access policies help ensure that only compliant devices can access company resources, whether they are BYOD or corporate-owned. By setting up conditional access, IT can apply a uniform security baseline across all devices.

3. **Communicate Privacy Standards for BYOD**: Make sure employees understand that their personal data will not be accessed on BYOD devices. By communicating these standards upfront, IT can reduce concerns about privacy while ensuring users are aware of the policies that apply to their devices.

4. **Leverage Supervision Mode for Corporate Devices**: Enable supervision mode on corporate-owned devices to gain additional control over functionality. This feature is particularly useful for enforcing compliance in high-security environments, where IT needs enhanced visibility and control.

5. **Implement Selective Wipes for BYOD**: In cases where employees leave the organization or no longer require access to corporate data, using selective wipes on BYOD devices removes only the corporate data and apps, preserving the user's personal content.

The flexibility to manage BYOD and corporate-owned devices differently allows organizations to support a wider range of work styles and device ownership models. For BYOD devices, Intune's app-based security helps protect corporate data without intruding on personal privacy, making employees feel more comfortable using their devices for work. For corporate-owned devices, Intune's full device management enables IT teams to enforce stricter controls, ensuring these devices are always compliant with security standards and optimized for productivity.

Differentiating management based on ownership type is a best practice for modern workplaces, providing the control needed for corporate security without sacrificing user experience. By aligning policies with the ownership model, IT teams can build a secure, flexible device environment that supports both employee preferences and organizational goals.

Best Practices for Enrollment

The enrollment process is the first interaction users have with Intune on their devices, making it a critical part of their experience with mobile device management. A smooth enrollment not only minimizes frustration but also sets the stage for consistent device compliance and security. For IT teams, effective enrollment processes streamline onboarding, reduce help desk requests, and establish a solid foundation for ongoing device management. By following best practices for enrollment, IT can ensure users have a simple, seamless experience while keeping security and management controls intact.

1. Choose the Right Enrollment Method for Each Device Type

As we've seen in previous sections, Intune offers different enrollment methods based on device ownership. Selecting the right method is key to simplifying the setup process and ensuring policies are applied correctly.

- **BYOD Devices**: For personal devices, use user-initiated enrollment. This approach limits management to specific apps, preserving user privacy and minimizing intrusiveness.

- **Corporate-Owned Devices**: For devices owned by the organization, automatic enrollment through Apple Business Manager (ABM) provides a zero-touch deployment experience. Users can power on their devices and automatically receive all configurations, apps, and security policies with minimal effort.

Choosing the appropriate enrollment method for each device type prevents confusion, builds trust with users, and ensures each device is managed according to organizational standards.

2. Pre-Configure Enrollment Profiles

Enrollment profiles define the initial setup and configuration of devices, allowing IT to pre-set important options like WiFi configurations, VPN settings, and security requirements. By creating and applying enrollment profiles for specific groups or departments, you can customize the setup experience to fit the unique needs of each role.

- **Skip Unnecessary Setup Steps**: Configure profiles to skip setup steps like Apple ID login, location services, and Siri setup, which aren't critical for work purposes. This saves time for users and reduces the number of steps required to get started.

- **Set Language and Region Defaults**: Defining language and region in advance can simplify the initial setup process, especially for organizations with employees in various locations.

Pre-configuring these options in enrollment profiles creates a more streamlined, efficient setup, helping users get up and running faster.

3. Communicate the Enrollment Process Clearly

For users who are unfamiliar with device management, enrollment can be a confusing process. Clear communication about what to expect, what permissions are needed, and why certain steps are required can significantly reduce user frustration and enrollment-related support requests.

- **Provide Step-by-Step Instructions**: Create a simple guide or FAQ that walks users through each step of the enrollment process. Include screenshots and clear explanations of why certain permissions (like location or camera access) are required for work apps.

- **Explain Privacy Protections for BYOD**: For BYOD enrollments, reassure users that Intune will not access personal data or monitor personal activity. This transparency builds trust and encourages users to complete the enrollment process without concerns about privacy.

By proactively communicating about the enrollment experience, IT can foster a positive relationship with users and reduce the likelihood of support requests related to the process.

4. Use Conditional Access Policies to Enforce Compliance

Conditional access policies ensure that only compliant devices can access company resources. These policies verify that enrolled devices meet minimum security standards, such as having the latest OS version or requiring a passcode, before granting access to apps and data. Implementing conditional access during enrollment helps establish a security baseline from the start.

- **Set Compliance Standards**: Define compliance requirements that devices must meet to access resources, including OS versions, security patches, and device encryption.

- **Require Multi-Factor Authentication (MFA)**: For added security, consider requiring MFA during enrollment to ensure that only authorized users are enrolling devices.

Conditional access policies create a secure entry point for all devices, safeguarding data and resources without disrupting the user experience.

5. Enable Custom Branding and User Messages

Adding custom branding to the enrollment experience can make it feel more professional and welcoming for users. By including your organization's logo, custom messages, and a friendly welcome screen, you create a more personalized experience.

- **Add Company Branding**: Use the Microsoft Endpoint Manager Admin Center to add your company logo and colors to the enrollment process. This touch reinforces a sense of connection and professionalism for users.

- **Create a Welcome Message**: A welcome message with basic information about the enrollment process and contact details for support can reassure users and encourage a smooth setup.

Branding elements create a cohesive experience and give users confidence that they're following an official company process.

6. Offer Support and Troubleshooting Resources

No matter how streamlined your enrollment process is, some users may still need assistance. Offering resources for common troubleshooting steps or providing contact information for support can help users resolve issues quickly and independently.

- **Create a Troubleshooting Guide**: Common issues, such as incorrect passwords or network connectivity problems, can be addressed in a simple troubleshooting guide. Include solutions for typical setup challenges to empower users to resolve issues on their own.

- **Provide IT Support Contact Information**: Make sure users know how to reach IT support if they encounter problems that they can't resolve themselves.

Providing these resources makes users feel supported and confident, reducing the likelihood of lengthy enrollment delays.

7. Perform Regular Testing and Review Enrollment Settings

Enrollment configurations should be periodically reviewed and tested to ensure they're up to date and aligned with current security practices. Regular testing helps identify any potential issues before they affect end users and allows IT to make adjustments as needed.

- **Test Enrollment Profiles with Sample Devices**: Whenever you update enrollment profiles or add new settings, test the changes on sample devices to verify they're working as expected.

- **Review Security and Compliance Policies**: Ensure that conditional access and compliance policies reflect the latest organizational security standards. Adjust policies if needed to address emerging threats or changes in regulatory requirements.

Routine testing and reviews keep the enrollment process smooth and effective, enhancing both security and user experience.

8. Automate Where Possible

Automation can greatly improve efficiency for IT and create a smoother experience for users. Leverage automation options within Intune to simplify routine enrollment tasks and minimize manual intervention.

- **Use Apple Business Manager for Automatic Enrollment**: For corporate-owned devices, enable automatic enrollment through ABM, allowing devices to be pre-configured without user involvement.

- **Automate App Deployment**: Configure Intune to automatically push required apps to devices as soon as they're enrolled. This approach ensures that users have the tools they need immediately upon setup.

Automation reduces the workload on IT teams, allowing them to focus on other critical tasks while ensuring that users receive a seamless experience.

A well-designed enrollment process benefits both IT and end users, creating a secure, efficient, and user-friendly experience. For IT, effective enrollment reduces help desk calls, ensures compliance, and provides peace of mind that devices are configured according to organizational standards. For users, a smooth enrollment experience minimizes the setup time, provides a clear path to access work resources, and fosters trust in IT's management approach.

Enrolling Devices with Ease

Alex glanced at his notebook, reviewing his list of key tasks for the day. At the top of the list, underlined twice, was the next stage of his Intune journey: enrolling iOS devices. His manager, Lucy, had emphasized that getting enrollment right was crucial—it was the moment users first experienced Intune on their devices, and a smooth setup could make all the difference in how well they accepted the new system. He wanted to make sure users could navigate the setup easily and, just as importantly, feel confident about using their devices for work.

Firing up his laptop, Alex flipped to the next module in his *Intune Playbook Companion Series* book. The chapter was all about enrollment—specifically, the choices between user-initiated enrollment for BYOD devices and automatic enrollment for corporate-owned devices. Each had its unique approach and set of considerations, and Alex was eager to dive into the differences.

The first concept, user-initiated enrollment, seemed straightforward. For BYOD (Bring Your Own Device) scenarios, users could kick off the process themselves by downloading the Company Portal app and signing in with their work credentials. Once they were logged in, the app would guide them through enrolling their device, securing work apps, and setting any necessary policies. As Alex imagined employees following these steps on their personal devices, he realized how important it would be to communicate clearly about privacy. He knew that some users might be nervous about enrolling their personal devices, concerned that IT would have access to their photos, messages, and private apps.

He made a note to suggest adding a privacy FAQ to the onboarding guide. The FAQ would reassure users that Intune's policies would only apply to work apps and that their personal data would remain untouched. For Alex, building trust with users seemed just as critical as configuring the devices correctly.

The chapter then shifted focus to automatic enrollment for corporate-owned devices. Here, the process was designed to be hands-off for users. By connecting Intune to Apple Business Manager (ABM), IT could ensure that company-issued devices were enrolled right out of the box. Alex liked the sound of "zero-touch deployment." It would mean that users could simply power on their new device, connect to WiFi, and immediately receive all the necessary apps and settings. He imagined the experience for new hires, turning on their company iPhones for the first time and seeing it load up with everything they needed, no extra steps required. It sounded like a great way to make them feel welcomed and ready to start.

His excitement grew as he dove into the next section: best practices for a smooth enrollment experience. The tips seemed simple but packed a punch. One of his favorites was the idea of pre-configuring enrollment profiles. By setting up profiles that skipped unnecessary setup steps like Apple ID login and Siri, IT could simplify the process, saving users valuable time. He pictured himself streamlining the setup for different departments, with customized profiles for roles like sales, support, and management. For him, these tweaks would make the enrollment feel more personal, almost like rolling out a customized welcome mat for each user.

Then, he saw a note about adding custom branding to the enrollment experience, and Alex perked up. With the right logo and a short welcome message, he could make the setup feel professional and reassuring. It was a small detail, but he knew that touches like these mattered. Users would be more likely to trust the process if it felt like an official part of the company.

Finally, the chapter touched on conditional access policies, something that Lucy had mentioned would be a "game-changer" for device security. These policies would ensure that only compliant devices could access company resources, verifying things like OS version and passcode settings before letting users into sensitive apps. It was a security measure that worked in the background, protecting data without disrupting users. He made a mental note to talk to Lucy about setting up these policies to make sure they were just right for their organization's needs.

By the time Alex closed his laptop for the day, he felt like he had a solid grasp on enrollment. He had a plan, a set of best practices to follow, and a newfound respect for the balance between IT control and user experience. The BYOD vs. corporate-owned approach made so much sense now—each with its unique path that allowed for the right level of control without overstepping.

Before heading out, Alex drafted a checklist for setting up his first round of enrollment profiles, keeping in mind everything he'd learned. He could already feel the excitement of seeing it all come together. Tomorrow, he'd start setting up test devices, running through the enrollment process himself to make sure it was as smooth as possible for users. There was still a lot to learn, but each step was another building block, bringing him closer to mastering iOS device management with Intune.

As he left the office, he couldn't help but think about what came next. With enrollment nearly in place, he'd soon dive into configuring policies for security and compliance—a whole new layer to explore. But for now, he was ready for the next challenge, confident and equipped with the knowledge to make enrollment a seamless experience for everyone.

Will Alex's new enrollment configurations stand up to testing?

Summary and Reflection

Enrolling iOS devices into Intune is a pivotal step in creating a secure, manageable, and user-friendly device environment. In this chapter, we explored the two main options for enrollment: user-initiated enrollment for BYOD (Bring Your Own Device) scenarios and automatic enrollment for corporate-owned devices. Each method offers unique advantages and considerations, allowing IT teams to tailor the enrollment process to different user needs and device types.

We also covered essential best practices for enrollment, from choosing the right method for each device type to configuring enrollment profiles, setting conditional access policies, and adding custom branding for a personalized experience. These best practices help ensure that users have a smooth setup experience while keeping security standards intact.

For organizations, a seamless enrollment process is a key component in gaining user trust and ensuring consistent device compliance. By implementing thoughtful enrollment practices, IT teams not only reduce the time spent on support requests but also build a strong foundation for ongoing management and security.

As we followed Alex's journey in this chapter, we saw him dive into the complexities of enrolling devices in Intune, learning to balance the requirements of both BYOD and corporate-owned devices. For Alex, the process was a mix of learning technical skills and understanding user experience. He quickly discovered that enrollment wasn't just about configuring devices; it was about creating a sense of trust and comfort for users, especially those using personal devices for work.

Just like Alex, your journey through iOS device management will involve making decisions that impact both the technical and human aspects of device enrollment. You'll face challenges around choosing the right enrollment methods, customizing profiles, and finding ways to make the process as intuitive as possible for users. And as Alex realized, users will appreciate clear communication about what Intune can and cannot access on their devices—particularly for BYOD users concerned about their privacy.

Alex's attention to detail in customizing enrollment profiles and adding branding reflects the real-world impact of small touches in IT management. By taking the time to personalize and simplify the enrollment experience, you can create a welcoming, professional environment for your users. They're more likely to embrace Intune and follow best practices when they feel that the system is designed with their experience in mind.

As you continue on your journey, remember that each step Alex took—from understanding BYOD vs. corporate-owned devices to adding conditional access and customization—is also available to you. These are tools that not only enhance your technical skills but also help you support users and protect company resources in a way that feels effortless to them.

Enrollment is just the beginning. Now that your devices are set up in Intune, you're ready to dive deeper into configuring policies for security and compliance. Just as Alex anticipates learning how to keep devices secure while empowering users, you too will gain insights into how Intune can enforce device policies, protect corporate data, and maintain regulatory compliance.

Alex's journey continues, and so does yours—toward a fully equipped, secure, and user-friendly Intune environment for managing iOS devices.

Configuring Policies for iOS Devices

In today's security-focused landscape, managing compliance is a key responsibility for IT administrators. Compliance policies in Microsoft Intune are a critical tool that helps ensure that all devices accessing company resources meet specific security standards. For iOS devices, compliance policies enforce a set of rules that devices must follow to access corporate data, helping to protect sensitive information and maintain a consistent security posture across your organization.

In Intune, compliance refers to a device's adherence to a set of defined security requirements. Compliance policies are designed to evaluate each device's configuration and determine if it meets the required criteria. For instance, policies can enforce settings like minimum OS versions, password requirements, encryption standards, and security patches. If a device doesn't comply with these requirements, Intune can restrict its access to corporate resources until it meets the necessary standards.

Compliance policies are particularly valuable for enforcing security on mobile devices like iPhones and iPads, which often travel outside the controlled environment of an office. By ensuring each device follows security guidelines, IT administrators can mitigate risks such as unauthorized access, data leakage, and exposure to vulnerabilities. For organizations that must adhere to strict regulatory requirements, compliance policies also help demonstrate a commitment to data protection and security best practices.

When a device is non-compliant, Intune can trigger actions like notifying the user, restricting access, or requiring specific updates. This functionality allows IT to balance security with user flexibility, providing a way for users to correct issues while protecting the organization's resources.

Setting up compliance policies in Intune for iOS devices is straightforward, with customizable options that can be tailored to meet your organization's specific needs. Here's a step-by-step guide to creating a basic compliance policy in Intune for iOS devices.

Step 1: Access the Compliance Policies in Microsoft Endpoint Manager

1. Open the Microsoft Endpoint Manager Admin Center and sign in with your administrator credentials.

2. From the main dashboard, navigate to Devices > iOS/iPadOS > Compliance.

3. Select Create Policy to start setting up a new compliance policy for iOS devices.

This section in Endpoint Manager is where you can manage all compliance policies, create new ones, and modify existing ones for iOS devices.

Step 2: Define the Basic Settings for the Compliance Policy

1. Enter a name and optional description for the policy. For instance, you might name it "iOS Basic Compliance Policy" to keep it distinct from other policies.

2. Choose iOS/iPadOS as the platform to specify that the policy applies to iOS devices.

3. In the Compliance settings area, you'll see several categories where you can configure the policy requirements, such as device health, password requirements, and system security.

Each compliance policy should be named clearly to make it easier to locate and modify as your needs evolve. Descriptive names can also help with reporting, as you'll be able to quickly identify which policies are being applied to different groups or roles.

Step 3: Configure Compliance Requirements

Under Compliance settings, you'll configure specific rules that devices must follow. Here are a few common compliance settings to consider for iOS devices:

- **Password Requirements**: Enforce minimum password requirements to ensure that devices are secure. For instance, you can require a six-digit passcode, prohibit simple passcodes, and specify the number of failed attempts allowed before the device is locked.

- **Device Health**: Require that devices are not jailbroken. This setting is essential for protecting corporate data, as jailbroken devices bypass Apple's built-in security features and are more vulnerable to unauthorized access.

- **Minimum OS Version**: Set a minimum iOS version that devices must have to be considered compliant. This ensures that all devices have the latest security patches and updates from Apple.

- **Encryption**: Enable device encryption to protect stored data, making it harder for unauthorized users to access sensitive information if the device is lost or stolen.

By configuring these settings, you create a compliance policy that enforces core security requirements on each device. You can customize each requirement to suit your organization's security posture, striking a balance between stringent protection and usability.

Step 4: Assign the Compliance Policy to Device Groups

Once the compliance policy is configured, the next step is to assign it to specific device groups within your organization.

1. In the Assignments section of the policy creation wizard, choose the device groups that should receive this policy. For example, you might assign it to "All Corporate iOS Devices" or "Sales Team iOS Devices."

2. Assigning policies by group allows for more granular control, enabling you to create tailored policies for different teams or departments if needed.

Device group assignments make it easy to apply compliance policies to multiple devices at once, ensuring consistency across your organization.

Step 5: Configure Actions for Non-Compliance

After assigning the policy, configure actions to be taken when a device is found to be non-compliant. Intune provides several options for handling non-compliance, allowing you to set responses based on the severity of the issue.

- **Notify User**: Send a notification to the user, informing them of the non-compliance issue and the steps needed to resolve it.

- **Restrict Access**: Temporarily restrict the device's access to corporate resources until it becomes compliant.

- **Mark Device as Non-Compliant**: Flag the device in the system, which may trigger additional actions based on conditional access policies.

Non-compliance actions are designed to encourage users to bring their devices back into compliance while protecting corporate resources in the meantime. For example, sending a notification can be a gentle reminder, while restricting access serves as a stronger incentive to resolve the issue promptly.

Configuring compliance policies effectively can improve security while ensuring minimal disruption for users. Here are some best practices to keep in mind:

- **Start with Basic Policies**: Begin with essential settings like password requirements and device health checks. Over time, you can adjust and expand policies as needed.

- **Educate Users About Compliance**: Inform users about the importance of compliance policies and explain what they can do to maintain compliance. Providing clear guidance helps reduce confusion and support requests.

- **Review and Update Policies Regularly**: Periodically review compliance policies to ensure they're up to date with current security standards and organizational needs. Updating policies can help address new threats and ensure continued protection.

Compliance policies are a cornerstone of effective device management. By ensuring that each device follows a consistent set of security rules, IT can protect corporate data, maintain control over device health, and minimize vulnerabilities. For end users, compliance policies also establish clear expectations, helping them understand the security requirements needed to access corporate resources.

Device Configuration Policies: Setting Up WiFi, Email, VPN, and Other Configurations

Device configuration policies in Microsoft Intune enable IT administrators to pre-configure essential settings on iOS devices, allowing users to connect seamlessly to organizational resources without manual setup. These policies allow you to push configurations for WiFi, email, VPN, and more, creating a consistent, ready-to-use environment for all devices. By automating these configurations, IT can save time, reduce support requests, and ensure that devices are aligned with organizational standards from day one.

Device configuration policies are crucial for both security and user experience. When users receive devices pre-configured with network, email, and VPN settings, they can start working immediately without navigating setup steps. This improves efficiency, minimizes potential setup errors, and enhances security by ensuring all devices connect through approved configurations.

Pre-configured policies also allow IT to enforce consistent settings across all devices, reducing the variability and potential security risks associated with manually configured devices. For example, standardizing VPN configurations ensures that all connections to corporate resources are secure, while pre-setting WiFi settings ensures devices connect to trusted networks only.

WiFi configuration policies allow IT to automatically connect iOS devices to specific WiFi networks, ensuring secure access to corporate resources and reducing reliance on unapproved networks.

1. Open the Microsoft Endpoint Manager Admin Center and go to Devices > iOS/iPadOS > Configuration.

2. Click Create Profile and select iOS/iPadOS as the platform, then choose WiFi as the profile type.

3. In the configuration wizard, provide the following settings:

   o **Network Name (SSID)**: Enter the WiFi network name (SSID) that devices should connect to.

   o **Connection Type**: Choose the connection type, such as WPA/WPA2-Personal or WPA2-Enterprise, depending on your network's security requirements.

   o **Password**: If using a secured WiFi, enter the network password to automatically connect devices to the network.

   o **EAP Type (for WPA2-Enterprise)**: If using WPA2-Enterprise, select the EAP type required for authentication, such as PEAP or TLS.

4. Assign the WiFi Configuration to the relevant device groups. For example, you might assign it to all iOS devices within the corporate network or specific groups that require WiFi access in office spaces.

With a WiFi policy, users can automatically connect to secure networks without needing to know passwords or manually select networks, improving security and convenience.

Email configuration policies allow you to pre-configure email accounts on iOS devices, streamlining access to corporate email and ensuring that users can securely communicate with colleagues.

1. In Endpoint Manager, go to Devices > iOS/iPadOS > Configuration Profiles and select Create Profile.

2. Choose iOS/iPadOS as the platform, then select Email as the profile type.

3. Configure the following settings for the email profile:

   o **Email Server**: Enter the email server address, typically in the format outlook.office365.com for Office 365 or based on your organization's email server.

   o **Account Name**: Define the account name as it will appear on users' devices.

   o **Username and Email Address**: Use dynamic variables such as {{userprincipalname}} to automatically assign usernames and email addresses, ensuring that each device receives personalized configurations.

   o **Authentication Method**: Specify the authentication method, such as username and password or certificate-based authentication.

   o **Sync Settings**: Set the sync behavior for calendar, contacts, notes, and tasks.

4. Assign the Email Profile to appropriate device groups, such as specific departments or employees who need access to corporate email on mobile.

This policy removes the need for manual email setup and ensures all devices access corporate email securely and consistently, minimizing configuration errors and support calls.

VPN configuration policies allow devices to securely connect to corporate resources from remote locations, essential for mobile users accessing sensitive data outside of secure networks.

1. In Endpoint Manager, navigate to Devices > iOS/iPadOS > Configuration Profiles and select Create Profile.

2. Choose iOS/iPadOS as the platform and VPN as the profile type.

3. Configure the following VPN settings:

   o **Connection Name**: Define a name for the VPN connection, such as "Corporate VPN."

   o **Server Address**: Enter the VPN server address provided by your organization's VPN provider.

   o **Authentication Method**: Choose the authentication method, such as username and password, certificate, or shared secret.

   o **Automatic VPN Connection**: Enable this setting if you want devices to connect to VPN automatically when accessing specific domains or resources.

   o **Custom VPN Settings**: Some VPN providers may require additional custom configurations, which can be added in this section.

4. **Assign the VPN Profile** to device groups that require remote access to corporate networks, such as remote employees or field teams.

Pre-configuring VPN settings helps ensure that all devices connect securely to corporate resources, supporting secure data access for remote and mobile users without manual VPN setup.

In addition to WiFi, email, and VPN, Intune allows you to configure several other settings to enhance usability and security for iOS devices:

- **App Configuration Policies**: Set up specific settings within managed apps (like Outlook or Teams) to customize app behavior, streamline login, or control app permissions.

- **Device Restrictions**: Control specific device features, such as restricting access to the App Store, disabling screen capture, or blocking certain apps. Device restrictions are particularly useful for corporate-owned devices where stricter controls are appropriate.

- **Certificate Profiles**: Deploy certificates to authenticate devices on WiFi or VPN networks without relying on passwords. Certificate profiles improve security by enabling seamless authentication for devices on protected networks.

These additional configurations allow IT to further customize the iOS experience, enabling or restricting functionality based on organizational requirements. They also help maintain security standards by limiting access to non-approved apps and resources.

Once all configuration policies are created, assigning them to device groups is essential to enforce settings across the organization. Assign each policy to relevant groups (e.g., "All Corporate iOS Devices" or "Remote Teams") to ensure the right settings are applied to the right users.

Testing policies on sample devices is also a good practice. Testing allows you to verify that configurations are applied correctly and that users can connect without issues. It's helpful to enlist feedback from a small group of users to identify any adjustments needed before rolling out policies organization-wide.

Device configuration policies streamline connectivity and improve user productivity by eliminating the need for manual setups. They also strengthen security by ensuring all devices connect through approved settings and limiting access to corporate resources. By managing essential configurations centrally, IT can enforce consistent standards, simplify onboarding for new devices, and reduce the risk of configuration errors that could lead to security vulnerabilities.

App Protection Policies

App protection policies (APP) in Microsoft Intune provide an additional layer of security by protecting data within specific apps, rather than the entire device. These policies are especially valuable in Bring Your Own Device (BYOD) scenarios, where users need access to work apps on personal devices, as well as on corporate-owned devices. By focusing on app-level security, Intune allows IT to control how data is accessed, shared, and stored within managed applications, ensuring that corporate information remains protected without impacting personal data.

In a mobile-first world, many employees access corporate data on personal devices, which can present security challenges. App protection policies in Intune allow IT administrators to control data within specific work-related apps without having to manage the device itself. These policies define how data can be used, shared, and stored, enforcing security measures such as encryption, authentication, and data protection. This approach enables organizations to maintain data security, even on devices not fully managed by Intune.

App protection policies also help ensure compliance with organizational security standards by restricting data sharing between work and personal apps, preventing unauthorized access, and enabling selective wipe capabilities that remove only work-related data from a device if necessary. These policies create a secure environment that supports both productivity and data protection.

App protection policies in Intune include various settings to manage how users can interact with corporate data within managed apps. Here are some of the core options you can configure:

- **Data Transfer Controls**: Restrict the sharing of data between managed (work) and unmanaged (personal) apps. For example, you can prevent users from copying data from a work email account to a personal messaging app.

- **Encryption**: Require data encryption within managed apps to ensure data remains secure even if the device is lost or stolen.

- **Access Requirements**: Set requirements for accessing managed apps, such as requiring a PIN or biometric authentication (Face ID or Touch ID) to open an app containing work data.

- **Data Wipe and Protection**: Configure policies to automatically wipe work data from an app after a certain period of inactivity or if the user fails repeated login attempts.

These settings enable IT to enforce consistent data protection standards, ensuring that corporate information remains within approved, managed apps and is not exposed to unauthorized access.

Step-by-Step Guide to Setting Up App Protection Policies for iOS Devices

Setting up app protection policies in Intune for iOS devices is straightforward and highly customizable, with options to apply policies to specific apps and user groups. Here's a step-by-step guide to creating a basic app protection policy for iOS devices.

Step 1: Access the App Protection Policies in Microsoft Endpoint Manager

1. Open the Microsoft Endpoint Manager Admin Center and sign in with your administrator credentials.

2. Navigate to Apps > App Protection Policies.

3. Click Create Policy to start creating a new app protection policy for iOS devices.

This area of Endpoint Manager is where you can create, manage, and modify app protection policies for iOS and other platforms.

Step 2: Define the Policy Basics

1. Enter a name and optional description for the policy, such as "iOS App Protection for Corporate Data" to distinguish it from other policies.

2. Choose iOS/iPadOS as the platform to specify that the policy applies to iOS devices.

3. In the Targeted apps section, select the apps you want this policy to protect. Commonly managed apps include Outlook, OneDrive, Teams, and other Office apps.

Choosing specific apps allows you to control how data within these apps is accessed and shared, ensuring data security for the most commonly used work applications.

Step 3: Configure Data Protection Settings

Data protection settings are the core of app protection policies. These settings control how users can interact with data within managed apps:

- **Prevent Data Transfer to Unmanaged Apps**: Enable this setting to restrict data sharing to only managed apps, preventing users from copying data from work apps to personal apps.

- **Restrict Save-As**: Block the ability to save copies of documents to non-managed locations, such as personal cloud storage or third-party apps.

- **Encrypt App Data**: Ensure all data within the managed app is encrypted, securing it against unauthorized access if the device is lost or stolen.

These data protection settings help enforce strict boundaries between corporate and personal data, ensuring that sensitive information stays within secure, managed apps.

Step 4: Set Access Requirements

Access requirements control how users authenticate to access managed apps, ensuring that only authorized users can open apps containing work data.

- **Require PIN for Access**: Set a requirement for users to enter a PIN each time they access the app. This adds an extra layer of security on top of device authentication.

- **Use Biometric Authentication**: Allow biometric options like Face ID or Touch ID for app access, providing a quick and secure login method.

- **Block Jailbroken Devices**: Prevent access to managed apps on jailbroken devices, as these devices have reduced security protections.

By enforcing access requirements, you can ensure that only verified users can access work data within managed apps, enhancing data security.

Step 5: Configure Conditional Data Wipe

Conditional data wipe settings enable IT to define conditions under which corporate data should be automatically wiped from the app. This is particularly useful in scenarios where devices may be lost, stolen, or left inactive for long periods.

- **Offline Interval**: Specify the maximum time a device can be offline before the app data is automatically wiped. For example, you might set a 30-day limit for inactive devices.

- **Failed Authentication Attempts**: Define the number of failed login attempts allowed before work data is wiped. This is a useful setting to prevent unauthorized access to work data.

Data wipe settings ensure that corporate data remains secure, even if a device becomes inaccessible or compromised.

Step 6: Assign the App Protection Policy to User Groups

Finally, assign the app protection policy to specific user groups within your organization.

1. In the **Assignments** section, select the **user groups** you want to apply the policy to. For example, you might assign it to "All Employees" or specific departments such as "Sales Team."

2. Review and confirm the settings, then save the policy.

Assigning app protection policies by user group allows for flexibility and ensures that only users with work data access are subject to these security measures.

To make the most of app protection policies, consider the following best practices:

- **Use Dynamic Targeting for Apps**: Target commonly used apps across the organization, such as Outlook and Teams, to ensure consistent data protection for all users.

- **Educate Users About Policy Requirements**: Explain the importance of app protection policies and how they safeguard corporate data. Providing a clear understanding helps users comply with policies and reduces potential confusion.

- **Test Policies with a Pilot Group**: Before deploying app protection policies organization-wide, test them with a small group to ensure settings function as expected and don't interfere with usability.

These practices help ensure that app protection policies are effective and well-received, improving both security and user experience.

App protection policies enable organizations to protect corporate data at the application level, without needing full device control. This is particularly valuable in BYOD scenarios, where users expect a degree of privacy on personal devices. By applying app-level security, Intune ensures that work data remains safe and secure, reducing the risk of data breaches, unauthorized access, and accidental data loss.

Securing the Essentials

Alex tapped his pen on his desk, reading over his notes on app protection policies. His goal for the day was to understand how these policies could lock down corporate data within specific apps on iOS devices, like Outlook, Teams, and OneDrive. It was different from the device-wide management he'd been studying. App protection policies didn't control the whole device—they focused on securing only the apps that contained work data. For Alex, this idea of app-level security was a revelation. It meant he could protect company information without having to manage every corner of an employee's device.

The concept made sense, especially when it came to BYOD (Bring Your Own Device). As he thought back to Lucy's reminders about user privacy, he saw how app protection policies could bridge the gap. Instead of needing control over the entire phone, Intune could control just the parts that mattered for work. Personal photos, messages, and other apps would stay private—untouched by IT. Alex could see how this approach would make employees more comfortable with enrolling their devices.

He turned his attention to the Intune Playbook Series book, where the next section walked through core settings for app protection. The first step was data transfer controls, which limited data sharing between managed (work) apps and unmanaged (personal) apps. As Alex read about preventing data from being copied from Outlook to a personal messaging app, he jotted down a note: *"Keeps work data from leaking into personal apps."* It was a simple setting but one that could save the company from accidental data loss.

The next setting was encryption. This would ensure that any data within the managed apps was encrypted, even on a personal device. Alex imagined the scenario: an employee's phone goes missing. Thanks to app protection policies, any work data inside managed apps like Outlook or Teams would stay secure, encrypted and safe from prying eyes. He appreciated how this setting didn't require the user to do anything— Intune would handle it automatically, adding a layer of security behind the scenes.

Alex moved on to access requirements and saw options for requiring users to enter a PIN or use Face ID or Touch ID to access managed apps. As he clicked through the setup in Intune, he thought about how much security had evolved. These weren't just passwords and locks on devices; it was security woven into the apps, triggered every time a user opened Outlook or Teams. He imagined the experience for employees: they would simply look at their phone, and the app would open. But underneath, Intune was working to ensure that only authorized users could get to the data.

The book then introduced conditional data wipe, which intrigued him the most. He saw settings that allowed IT to wipe work data from an app if the device was inactive for too long or if someone repeatedly failed to log in. For Alex, it was the perfect safety net. If a device went offline or was compromised, Intune would act as a safeguard, removing corporate data before anyone could misuse it. He pictured a real-world scenario: a field employee's phone is stolen, and the thief tries to access their work apps. After a few failed attempts, Intune would step in, wiping all work-related data without affecting anything personal.

Excited to try it out, Alex decided to create a test app protection policy for a few apps, targeting Outlook, Teams, and OneDrive. He set it up to restrict data transfer, encrypt data, and require Face ID to open the app. He configured a conditional data wipe if someone entered an incorrect passcode five times in a row, thinking of it as a final layer of defense. After saving the settings, he assigned the policy to a test group, curious to see how it would work on an actual device.

After assigning the policy, Alex reviewed his setup, realizing how far he'd come. At first, device management had seemed like a matter of setting basic policies across the board. But now, he was learning to apply more targeted measures, balancing protection with usability. App protection policies didn't just lock down devices—they made it possible for users to work securely on their own terms, even on their own devices.

As he closed his laptop for the day, he felt a sense of accomplishment. Each setting he'd configured represented a layer of security that Intune could provide, all without disrupting the user experience. These policies were designed to protect corporate data, yes, but they also protected employees' privacy—a balance that Alex now understood was key to building trust with users.

Tomorrow, he would dive into other policies, more powerful tools for controlling access to corporate resources. But for now, he was satisfied, knowing he'd set up a system that kept data safe within the apps that mattered most.

Will Alex's app protection policies hold up under real-world testing?

Summary and Reflection

In this chapter, we explored three core components of Intune that help secure and manage iOS devices: compliance policies, device configuration policies, and app protection policies. Each of these policy types addresses different aspects of device management, from enforcing basic security standards to configuring connectivity settings and protecting data within specific apps.

Compliance policies help ensure that devices meet security requirements, such as minimum OS versions and password standards, before they can access corporate resources. These policies establish a baseline of security that every device must meet, making it easier for IT teams to manage a compliant, secure fleet of devices.

Device configuration policies streamline the user experience by pre-configuring essential settings like WiFi, VPN, and email, allowing users to access corporate resources with minimal setup. These policies enhance productivity and security by ensuring all devices connect through approved, secure configurations, reducing support calls and setup time.

App protection policies provide app-level security for corporate data, particularly valuable in BYOD scenarios. By controlling data access, transfer, and encryption within specific apps, Intune protects sensitive information without requiring full device management. This approach maintains user privacy while safeguarding corporate data, allowing for flexible, secure work on both corporate-owned and personal devices.

Together, these policies create a comprehensive framework for managing iOS devices, balancing security with usability and adapting to various device ownership models. This flexibility is essential for modern, mobile workplaces, where employees need secure, reliable access to corporate data from different devices and locations.

We followed Alex as he tackled each policy type, learning to configure and deploy settings that would support a secure and user-friendly environment for his organization's iOS devices. Alex's journey through compliance policies, device configurations, and app protection reflected the challenges many IT professionals face in balancing security needs with user experience.

For Alex, understanding compliance policies meant realizing that security isn't just about enforcing rules—it's about setting a baseline that keeps everyone's data safe. His work in configuring device settings highlighted the importance of simplifying connectivity and access for users, ensuring they could get to work quickly and securely without unnecessary obstacles. And as he dove into app protection policies, he saw how data security could be maintained within specific apps, allowing him to protect corporate data on personal devices while respecting user privacy.

In many ways, Alex's journey mirrors your own experience as you build out your Intune environment. Like Alex, you've learned to think critically about each policy type, understanding that Intune is not just a tool for enforcing rules but also for creating a supportive, efficient workspace. By following these steps, you're establishing a secure environment that respects both organizational requirements and user needs—a balance that is essential in today's mobile, flexible workplaces.

With compliance, configuration, and app protection policies in place, the next step is to explore conditional access policies. These policies add another layer of security by controlling who can access corporate resources based on device compliance, user identity, and location. As Alex moves forward with conditional access, he'll learn how to enforce even tighter security, ensuring that only authorized, secure devices can connect to sensitive data.

Alex's journey continues, and so does yours, toward building a robust, responsive, and secure Intune environment.

Deploying Apps to iOS Devices

Selecting the right apps for deployment is a key part of managing iOS devices with Intune. By strategically deploying essential Microsoft, company-specific, and third-party apps, IT can ensure that employees have the tools they need to be productive while keeping the environment secure and consistent. Microsoft Intune provides flexible options for deploying various types of apps, allowing IT teams to control app access, updates, and security on all managed devices.

Microsoft apps are often at the core of business operations, providing tools for communication, collaboration, productivity, and data management. Commonly deployed Microsoft apps for iOS include Outlook, Teams, OneDrive, Word, Excel, and PowerPoint. These apps are already integrated into the Microsoft 365 ecosystem, making them a natural fit for organizations that rely on Microsoft services.

Microsoft apps are designed to work seamlessly with Microsoft 365 services, providing a cohesive experience across devices and platforms. Deploying Microsoft apps through Intune allows IT to manage app settings, enforce security policies, and keep apps up to date, reducing the need for manual installation and updates by end users.

By deploying these apps, IT can ensure:

- **Consistency in Productivity Tools**: Employees have access to the same tools across different devices, promoting a standardized workflow and making it easier to collaborate.

- **Enhanced Security and Compliance**: Microsoft apps integrate with Intune and Microsoft 365 security features, supporting data protection through app protection policies and conditional access controls.

- **Centralized Updates and Support**: IT can control app versions and deploy updates as they become available, minimizing compatibility issues and ensuring all users have access to the latest features.

When deploying Microsoft apps, consider user roles and access requirements. For example, frontline workers may only need access to Outlook and Teams, while office-based staff might benefit from the full suite of Office apps. Tailoring Microsoft app deployment to different user groups enhances productivity and avoids unnecessary resource use.

Company-specific apps are often tailored to the unique needs of an organization. These can include custom apps developed in-house, apps configured with specific settings or branding, and line-of-business (LOB) applications that facilitate essential tasks, such as CRM (Customer Relationship Management) or ERP (Enterprise Resource Planning) systems.

Deploying company apps ensures that employees have access to the essential, custom tools that support daily business operations. These apps are typically unique to your organization's workflows and provide capabilities not available through standard, off-the-shelf solutions.

Benefits of deploying company apps include:

- **Streamlined Workflows**: Custom apps often align closely with business processes, helping employees complete tasks more efficiently.

- **Enhanced Branding**: Custom-branded apps reinforce your organization's identity and create a consistent experience for users.

- **Business-Critical Functionality**: Company apps may provide features tailored to specific operational needs, from logistics to sales support.

When deploying company apps, ensure that they are compatible with iOS and meet your organization's security standards. Use app protection policies to secure company data within these apps, and monitor performance to address any issues that could impact productivity.

Regular updates and maintenance are essential, as custom apps may require adjustments to stay compatible with iOS updates.

To deploy a company app through Intune, upload the app package (such as an IPA file for iOS) to Intune and specify deployment settings, including which user groups will receive the app. Intune allows you to set installation options such as required, available for enrolled devices, or uninstall—giving IT flexibility in how apps are deployed and managed.

Approved third-party apps are applications developed by external vendors that have been vetted and authorized by your organization. These might include productivity tools, project management apps, or industry-specific apps that support essential functions. Examples of popular third-party apps deployed by organizations include Zoom, Adobe Acrobat, Slack, and Salesforce.

Third-party apps extend the capabilities of iOS devices, providing tools that enhance collaboration, communication, and productivity. By selecting trusted, approved apps, IT can equip employees with additional resources while maintaining control over app security and compatibility.

Key benefits of deploying third-party apps include:

- **Increased Flexibility**: Third-party apps can address specialized needs or offer enhanced features that Microsoft or company apps may not provide.

- **User Familiarity**: Some third-party apps are widely used and familiar to employees, making adoption easier and reducing the need for training.

- **Integration with Workflows**: Many third-party apps integrate with other tools in the organization, such as CRM systems or productivity platforms, creating a more unified workflow.

When selecting third-party apps, ensure they meet security and compliance requirements. Vet each app carefully, looking at vendor reputation, data handling practices, and integration with your existing systems. Limit deployment to apps that have been reviewed and approved by IT, and consider applying app protection policies to secure data within these apps.

For third-party app deployment, Intune allows you to specify whether the app should be required (automatically installed on all assigned devices) or available for download in the Company Portal. Providing apps as "available" gives users the flexibility to download only the tools they need, while required apps ensure all users have access to essential resources.

Selecting the right mix of Microsoft, company, and third-party apps involves understanding user needs, security requirements, and business objectives. Here are some best practices to guide your app selection and deployment:

- **Create a Standardized App Suite**: Establish a set of core apps that all employees need, such as Outlook, Teams, and OneDrive. Standardizing a core suite helps streamline support and enhances collaboration.

- **Segment App Access by Role**: Tailor app deployment based on user roles and responsibilities. Different departments may have unique app requirements, so consider creating deployment groups based on team functions or job types.

- **Review and Update App Lists Regularly**: Periodically review the list of deployed apps to ensure they are up to date, relevant, and compliant with security standards. Remove any apps that are no longer needed to reduce clutter and improve performance.

- **Apply Security Controls Where Needed**: Use app protection policies and conditional access policies to enforce data security within critical apps, especially for BYOD devices or apps that handle sensitive data.

Selecting and deploying the right apps is essential for supporting user productivity while ensuring a secure, cohesive environment. By carefully choosing apps and managing their deployment through Intune, you can equip employees with the tools they need while maintaining control over data access and security.

App deployment is a key part of creating a well-rounded, productive mobile environment. By selecting the right combination of Microsoft, company, and third-party apps, IT teams can support diverse business needs while maintaining consistent control over app security and usage. Ensuring that employees have access to approved, up-to-date apps helps drive productivity and reduce security risks, setting the stage for a well-managed and secure iOS device ecosystem.

Required Apps vs. Available Apps

Microsoft Intune provides flexible deployment strategies to accommodate various app requirements across different user groups. When deploying apps to iOS devices, administrators can choose to push apps as required (automatically installed on all assigned devices) or as available (optional downloads from the Company Portal). Each deployment strategy has its own management style and benefits, allowing IT teams to tailor app access based on the needs of different users and roles.

Required apps are automatically installed on assigned devices without any action needed from users. These apps are essential for productivity, security, or compliance and ensure that all users have immediate access to critical tools. When an app is deployed as required, Intune pushes it to each device in the target group, making it accessible as soon as the device is enrolled or connected to Intune.

Required apps are best suited for applications that are critical to daily business operations, such as email clients, collaboration tools, and security-related applications. By automatically installing these apps, IT can streamline the onboarding process, reduce the need for manual app installation, and ensure that every user has access to the core tools needed to perform their role.

Examples of apps typically deployed as required include:

- **Microsoft Outlook** for email and calendar access

- **Microsoft Teams** for collaboration and communication

- **OneDrive** for secure file storage and sharing

- **VPN or security applications** to enforce secure access to corporate networks

Managing required apps involves ensuring that these critical tools are continuously available, up to date, and secure. Here's how IT can effectively manage required apps:

- **Monitor App Compliance and Updates**: Set Intune to push updates automatically to required apps. This keeps them aligned with the latest features, security patches, and compatibility improvements, minimizing the risk of security vulnerabilities.

- **Track Installation Success and Errors**: Regularly review app deployment reports in Intune to verify that required apps are installed on all target devices and to troubleshoot any errors.

- **Use Conditional Access and Compliance Policies**: For security-sensitive apps like VPN clients, enforce conditional access and compliance policies that restrict access unless the app is installed and configured correctly.

By automating deployment and monitoring compliance, required apps provide a secure and consistent environment where all users have access to essential tools.

Available apps, on the other hand, are not automatically installed but are made available for users to download from the Company Portal as needed. This deployment style offers flexibility, allowing users to choose apps based on their specific role or preferences while still ensuring access to approved, secure applications. Available apps appear in the Company Portal, where users can browse, select, and install them independently.

Available apps are ideal for applications that aren't essential for every user but may be necessary for certain roles, projects, or personal productivity. Making these apps available rather than required gives users the option to install them only when needed, reducing unnecessary installations and freeing up device resources.

Examples of apps typically deployed as available include:

- **Project Management Tools**: Tools like Trello or Asana may be useful for some teams but not required for everyone.

- **Specialized Software**: Industry-specific apps or tools for specialized tasks, such as design or analytics software.

- **Optional Productivity Tools**: Tools like Slack or Adobe Acrobat may enhance productivity for some users but are not required by all.

Managing available apps is more user-driven, providing users with control over which tools they want to download and install. This flexible approach can reduce the burden on IT and allows users to personalize their devices within approved guidelines.

- **Ensure Clear App Descriptions**: In the Company Portal, provide clear app descriptions and intended uses, helping users understand which apps are relevant to their roles.

- **Monitor Usage and Adoption**: Track app adoption rates to see which available apps are frequently downloaded. This can inform decisions about future app deployments or changes in the availability of certain tools.

- **Update and Remove Unused Apps Periodically**: Regularly review available apps to ensure they are up to date and relevant. Remove apps that are no longer used to declutter the Company Portal and maintain a streamlined app selection.

Available apps provide flexibility and empower users to customize their experience while giving IT the control to approve and monitor app installations.

The decision between deploying apps as required or available should align with each app's purpose, importance, and usage. Here are some key considerations when choosing the right deployment style:

- **Criticality to Daily Operations**: Apps essential for core tasks, such as email, storage, and communication, are best deployed as required to ensure every user has access from day one.

- **User Role and Function**: Tailor app deployment based on roles and departments. Sales teams might need CRM apps as required, while creative teams might need optional design tools.

- **Device Resources**: For devices with limited storage or processing power, consider using available apps for non-essential tools to prevent performance issues.

- **Flexibility and Personalization**: Available apps allow users to customize their devices with tools that enhance productivity, while required apps ensure consistency across all devices.

By understanding each app's purpose and how it fits into users' workflows, IT can create an effective deployment strategy that balances security, productivity, and personalization.

Implementing a successful app deployment strategy involves balancing organizational needs with user flexibility. Here are some best practices for deploying required and available apps in Intune:

- **Segment User Groups**: Create device groups based on user roles, departments, or functions. This makes it easy to assign required apps to specific teams while keeping optional tools available to those who need them.

- **Use Dynamic Targeting for Flexibility**: Consider dynamic user groups that automatically update based on criteria like job title or department. This allows you to adjust app deployment as users' roles change.

- **Provide Clear App Categories in the Company Portal**: Organize available apps by category, such as "Productivity,"

"Communication," and "Specialized Tools." This makes it easier for users to find relevant apps and encourages them to download tools that align with their needs.

- **Review and Optimize Regularly**: Periodically review required and available apps to ensure they are still relevant and effective. Remove apps that are no longer necessary or replace them with better alternatives to keep the app environment fresh and optimized.

A well-planned app deployment strategy enhances user experience, improves productivity, and helps maintain security. By deploying required apps that every user needs and offering available apps that provide optional tools, IT can strike a balance between control and flexibility. This approach ensures that all users have access to essential tools while also empowering them to personalize their devices with approved apps that support their individual roles.

Ensuring Apps Are Up-to-Date and Secure

Keeping apps up-to-date and secure is essential for maintaining a productive and protected mobile environment. Outdated apps can create security vulnerabilities, disrupt workflows, and introduce compatibility issues, especially with frequent iOS updates. Microsoft Intune provides robust tools for managing app updates and enforcing app protection policies to secure corporate data within approved applications.

App updates are crucial for several reasons. Regular updates typically include security patches that address vulnerabilities, feature improvements that enhance productivity, and compatibility adjustments that ensure apps work seamlessly with the latest iOS versions. Failure to update apps can expose the organization to security risks and lead to a poor user experience, especially if app functionality degrades due to outdated versions.

By managing updates through Intune, IT administrators can ensure that every user has access to the latest features and that corporate data remains secure within each app.

Managing app updates for iOS devices in Intune involves configuring settings that automate or enforce update processes, making it easier to keep apps current without requiring manual intervention from users.

1. **Automatic App Updates**: Enable automatic app updates for managed apps. This ensures that apps are always running the latest version, reducing the risk of security vulnerabilities and compatibility issues. For iOS, automatic updates can be configured through the App Store settings, while Intune can help monitor and enforce update compliance.

2. **Update Deployment Scheduling**: Schedule updates at times that minimize disruption to users. For example, you might schedule updates during off-peak hours or allow users a specific timeframe to update their apps. Providing a clear update window reduces the likelihood of disruptions and allows IT to manage app compliance proactively.

3. **Monitoring App Versions and Compliance**: Use Intune's reporting tools to track app versions and ensure compliance across all devices. Intune allows administrators to review which devices are running outdated app versions and push updates as needed. Monitoring app versions is especially important for required apps that may impact core productivity or security.

4. **Testing Updates in Stages**: For critical apps, consider testing updates with a pilot group before rolling them out organization-wide. A staged rollout helps identify any potential compatibility issues or bugs that could impact workflows, providing an opportunity to address these problems before the full deployment.

Managing app updates proactively keeps all users on the latest version, reducing security risks and improving overall productivity by ensuring users have access to the newest features and improvements.

App protection policies (APP) in Intune allow IT to safeguard data within managed apps, even if the devices themselves are not fully managed. These policies control how data is accessed, shared, and stored within specific apps, enforcing security measures that prevent data leaks and unauthorized access. App protection policies are especially valuable for BYOD scenarios, where users work on personal devices but access corporate data within approved apps.

Key app protection policy settings include:

- **Data Transfer Controls**: Restrict data transfer between managed (work) and unmanaged (personal) apps to prevent sensitive information from leaving approved channels. This ensures that corporate data remains within a secure environment.

- **Data Encryption**: Enforce data encryption within managed apps to protect sensitive information in case of device loss or theft. Encryption provides an additional layer of security, ensuring that data cannot be accessed without authorization.

- **Access Requirements**: Set requirements for accessing managed apps, such as requiring a PIN, biometric authentication, or device compliance checks. These settings enhance data security by ensuring that only authorized users can access corporate information within managed apps.

- **Conditional Data Wipe**: Configure policies that automatically wipe corporate data from apps if certain conditions are met, such as too many failed login attempts or extended inactivity. This feature protects corporate data in situations where the device may be lost, stolen, or compromised.

By applying app protection policies, IT administrators can control data security within specific apps, ensuring that sensitive information remains protected, even on personal or partially managed devices.

Combining app updates with app protection policies creates a comprehensive strategy that maintains both functionality and security. Here are some best practices to help you manage updates and enforce app protection policies effectively:

- **Enforce Regular Update Compliance**: Encourage users to keep apps up to date, especially those that handle corporate data. Use Intune's compliance policies to flag devices running outdated versions and notify users to update as needed.

- **Monitor and Adjust App Protection Policies**: Review app protection policies periodically to ensure they align with your organization's evolving security standards and operational needs. Adjust settings as necessary to address new security risks or compliance requirements.

- **Communicate Policy Requirements to Users**: Educate users on the importance of app protection policies and app updates, explaining how these measures protect both company data and their personal devices. A well-informed user base is more likely to comply with update and security requirements.

- **Integrate Conditional Access with App Protection**: Use conditional access policies in tandem with app protection policies to control app access based on factors like user location, device compliance, and app version. This approach further secures data by ensuring that only compliant, secure devices can access corporate resources.

- **Establish a Testing Process for App Updates**: For critical business apps, test updates with a small group of users before full deployment. This approach ensures updates are compatible and functional before rolling them out to the entire organization, reducing the risk of interruptions.

By combining effective update management with app protection policies, you create a secure environment where apps are not only current but also configured to protect corporate data at all times.

Managing updates and enforcing app protection policies are two essential components of a comprehensive mobile device security strategy. Keeping apps up to date minimizes vulnerabilities and compatibility issues, ensuring that all users have access to secure, reliable versions of essential tools. Meanwhile, app protection policies safeguard corporate data within each app, allowing IT to maintain security standards even in BYOD environments.

Together, these strategies create a balanced approach that supports both user productivity and data security, ensuring that apps remain functional, compliant, and secure throughout their lifecycle.

Tracking App Installations, Compliance, and Usage

Effective app deployment doesn't stop at installation; it also requires ongoing monitoring to ensure that apps remain compliant, up-to-date, and well-utilized. Microsoft Intune provides powerful reporting and analytics tools that allow IT administrators to track app installations, monitor compliance, and review app usage across managed devices. These insights enable proactive management, helping IT identify issues early, measure app adoption, and optimize the app ecosystem to better serve users.

Monitoring app deployment provides valuable insights into how apps perform within your organization and helps ensure that apps remain secure and effective for all users. By tracking metrics like installation status, compliance, and usage, IT can make data-driven decisions about which apps to continue supporting, update, or retire. Monitoring also allows IT teams to:

- **Identify Compliance and Security Gaps**: Quickly spot devices or users that haven't installed required apps or updated them to the latest version.

- **Optimize Resource Allocation**: Determine which apps are used most frequently and which might be unnecessary, helping streamline the app ecosystem and optimize device resources.

- **Enhance User Experience**: Address any issues with app performance or compatibility, ensuring that users have a seamless experience with their work tools.

- **Ensure Licensing and Compliance**: Ensure that apps are licensed correctly and are compliant with organizational and regulatory standards.

Intune provides real-time insights into the installation status of apps on managed devices, making it easy to see which apps are installed, pending, or facing errors. To track app installations:

1. Navigate to the Intune Admin Center and go to Apps > Monitor > App install status.

2. Select an app to view its installation summary, including the number of successful installations, pending installations, and installation failures.

For each installation, Intune provides detailed information, such as the affected devices, the error messages for failed installations, and the overall compliance rate. This data enables IT to identify and address installation issues, ensuring that required apps are available on all target devices.

Installation Status Categories

- **Installed**: Indicates successful installations, confirming that the app is available and ready for use on each device.

- **Not Installed**: Lists devices where the app is assigned but has not been installed, often due to connectivity issues or user actions.

- **Failed**: Provides details on any installation errors, helping IT troubleshoot issues and determine whether additional steps are needed.

Tracking app installations allows IT to maintain a complete picture of deployment status across the organization, ensuring that users have access to the tools they need.

Ensuring that apps are compliant with organizational security standards is critical for protecting data and maintaining control over the app environment. Intune provides compliance monitoring for apps, allowing IT to track whether devices meet necessary criteria, such as having the latest app version and security settings.

1. **Navigate to Compliance Reports**: In the Intune Admin Center, go to Reports > Device compliance to view an overview of compliance across managed devices.

2. **Review App-Specific Compliance**: For specific apps, such as those subject to strict data protection policies, use compliance policies to track settings like app version, encryption, and data access restrictions.

By monitoring app compliance, IT can quickly identify non-compliant devices and take action, such as pushing updates, enforcing app protection policies, or notifying users to correct the issue.

Intune's reporting features allow IT to gather insights into how frequently apps are used, which can inform decisions on app support, licensing, and resource allocation. Usage reports can show which apps are essential for productivity and which may be underutilized, providing a data-driven basis for optimizing the app environment.

While Intune does not directly track app usage frequency, integrating Intune data with Microsoft 365 usage analytics can offer insights into the adoption and active usage of core productivity apps like Teams, Outlook, and OneDrive.

1. **Use Microsoft 365 Admin Center**: For Microsoft apps, navigate to the Microsoft 365 Admin Center to access usage data and adoption trends.

2. **Identify Trends and Optimization Opportunities**: Analyze patterns to determine whether certain apps should be promoted,

better supported, or replaced based on how they are used by employees.

Understanding app usage patterns can help IT prioritize high-value tools and retire or reassign resources from underused apps, ensuring that users have the best possible tools for their needs.

Effective app monitoring and reporting require a proactive approach. Here are some best practices for keeping your app deployment secure, efficient, and aligned with organizational needs:

- **Set Up Regular Monitoring Cycles**: Establish a routine for reviewing app deployment reports, tracking installations, and checking compliance. Regular monitoring allows IT to catch issues early and address them before they impact productivity.

- **Utilize Alerts for Critical Events**: Configure alerts within Intune to notify IT of important events, such as failed app installations, compliance violations, or data wipe triggers. Alerts provide real-time updates, allowing IT to respond promptly to any issues.

- **Encourage User Feedback**: Solicit feedback from users on app performance and any challenges they encounter. Understanding user experiences helps IT identify potential improvements in app deployment and management.

- **Review and Adjust App Policies Regularly**: Periodically evaluate app protection, compliance, and deployment policies to ensure they are effective and aligned with your organization's current needs. Adjust policies as necessary to maintain security and compliance.

Monitoring and reporting on app deployment is essential for maintaining a secure and productive app environment. By tracking installations, compliance, and usage, IT can ensure that all deployed apps are current, functional, and secure. These insights help IT teams optimize the app ecosystem, proactively address issues, and support users effectively.

Using Intune's reporting and monitoring tools, IT can take a data-driven approach to app management, making adjustments as needed to improve both security and user experience. This continuous improvement process helps create a resilient, efficient mobile environment where users can rely on their apps to work seamlessly.

The App Deployment Challenge

Alex took a deep breath as he prepared to tackle one of the most anticipated parts of his Intune journey: deploying apps across iOS devices. This was where everything came together, from choosing the right apps to ensuring they stayed updated and secure. He understood that apps were at the core of user productivity—each app was a tool, a connection to resources, and often the foundation for employees' daily tasks. Getting deployment right meant more than just installing apps. It meant supporting users with seamless, secure, and up-to-date tools.

Sitting down with his notebook, Alex sketched out the types of apps his company relied on: the essential Microsoft apps, custom company-specific tools, and a few approved third-party apps. Each category had its own deployment strategy. The essentials, like Outlook, Teams, and OneDrive, were required; everyone needed these apps to stay connected. The custom apps were tailored for specific departments, and third-party apps like Zoom or Adobe Acrobat were more flexible—available for those who needed them but not forced on everyone.

He started by configuring required apps. He knew that setting these as required would ensure that everyone had access immediately, without needing to download them manually. As he set up Outlook, Teams, and OneDrive, he imagined the user experience: logging in on a new device and seeing everything already there, configured and ready to go. For Alex, this wasn't just about convenience—it was about creating a seamless entry point for new hires or users switching devices.

Once he'd finished with the essentials, he turned to the available apps. In Intune, he set Zoom, Adobe Acrobat, and a few other tools as "available" in the Company Portal. This would allow users to install them as needed. He liked the idea of providing flexibility, especially for roles with unique needs. He thought about the marketing and sales teams, who frequently used design tools, and the finance team, who often required specialized software. These groups could pick and choose what they needed, without having to scroll through a cluttered home screen.

With deployment configured, Alex's next step was setting up update and monitoring policies. He'd learned from his course that outdated apps were a common security vulnerability. By configuring Intune to automate app updates, he could ensure everyone had the latest version without them even noticing. Alex set the updates to roll out in stages, testing them with a pilot group before deploying them to the rest of the organization.

Next, he navigated to Intune's reporting tools to check his setup. From here, he could track which devices had installed the required apps, whether any installations had failed, and if certain apps were still pending. He noticed a handful of devices with installation errors and flagged them for troubleshooting. The data showed that most users had already downloaded the available apps they needed—a quick validation of the flexibility that made available apps so practical.

As he reviewed app compliance reports, he realized how useful the monitoring tools were. They allowed him to see not only who was up-to-date but also which devices were lagging in compliance. It gave him the insight he needed to keep apps secure across the board. He set up alerts for any critical app failures, compliance issues, or unexpected data wipes, knowing that real-time notifications would let him address problems as soon as they appeared.

At the end of the day, Alex took a moment to reflect. Deploying and monitoring apps had felt complex at first, but he'd found a rhythm. By automating updates, setting clear deployment strategies, and using the reporting tools, he felt like he'd built an efficient system for managing apps that balanced security, flexibility, and productivity.

Tomorrow, he'd move on to something new, he'd heard that this was where things got more advanced. But after seeing the power of Intune's deployment and monitoring capabilities, he felt ready for the challenge.

Will Alex's deployment strategy hold up as he introduces more advanced controls?

Summary and Reflection

We covered the essential components of deploying and managing apps on iOS devices with Intune. From selecting the right apps to deploying them efficiently and monitoring their performance, we explored strategies to create a productive and secure app environment for users.

We started by examining how to choose apps for deployment, including Microsoft apps, company-specific tools, and approved third-party apps. Each type of app serves different needs, and selecting the right mix ensures that users have access to the tools they require while maintaining security. Next, we looked at deployment strategies, differentiating between required apps, which are automatically installed on devices, and available apps, which users can choose to download from the Company Portal as needed. This flexibility supports diverse workflows and allows users to personalize their devices while meeting company standards.

We then discussed managing updates and app protection policies to keep apps up-to-date and secure. Regular updates reduce security risks and enhance functionality, while app protection policies enforce data security within individual apps, especially on BYOD devices. Finally, we explored monitoring and reporting on app deployment, using Intune's tools to track installation status, compliance, and usage, enabling IT to make data-driven decisions and promptly address any issues.

Together, these strategies create a comprehensive app deployment and management framework, ensuring that apps are deployed efficiently, updated regularly, and monitored for security and compliance. This approach not only supports productivity but also maintains a secure mobile environment.

We also followed Alex as he navigated the complexities of app deployment and monitoring. For Alex, deploying apps wasn't just a technical task; it was about understanding how each app fits into users' workflows and how to provide a seamless, secure experience. His careful approach to required and available apps reflects the importance of flexibility—balancing organizational control with user choice. Just as he configured essential apps for automatic deployment, he also empowered users by making optional tools available in the Company Portal.

Managing updates and setting up app protection policies was another critical step for Alex. He saw firsthand how regular updates and security controls within apps could protect company data without affecting personal devices. His work in monitoring app installations and tracking compliance taught him that deployment doesn't end at installation; it requires ongoing oversight and a proactive approach to ensure apps remain current and secure.

In many ways, Alex's journey mirrors your own. Whether you're setting up apps for the first time or refining an existing deployment, you've seen how important it is to approach app management holistically. Every app deployment decision, from required apps to update strategies, impacts the user experience, productivity, and security of your organization's mobile environment. Like Alex, you're learning to balance these elements, creating a reliable and user-friendly ecosystem where employees can work confidently with the tools they need.

With apps successfully deployed and managed, the next step in creating a secure mobile environment is to implement conditional access policies. These policies allow IT to control access to corporate resources based on factors like device compliance, user identity, and location, adding another layer of security that aligns access with organizational requirements.

Alex's journey continues, and so does yours—toward a fully optimized, secure, and productive Intune-managed environment.

Security and Compliance for iOS Devices

Conditional Access is a powerful feature in Microsoft Intune that provides IT administrators with granular control over who can access corporate resources, based on specific conditions. In today's mobile workforce, employees often access work data on devices outside the office, which can introduce security risks if not managed carefully. Conditional Access policies create a robust security framework by requiring that devices meet certain criteria before they're allowed access to sensitive resources. This helps protect corporate data, reduce unauthorized access, and enhance overall compliance.

Conditional Access is a security feature in Microsoft Azure Active Directory (Azure AD) that restricts access to applications and resources based on conditions such as user identity, device compliance, location, and more. When a user attempts to access a resource (like Office 365 apps or internal company applications), Conditional Access policies evaluate specific factors to determine whether the user should be granted access.

These factors include:

- **User Identity**: Ensures that only authorized users can access corporate resources.

- **Device Compliance**: Verifies that the device meets security requirements, such as being enrolled in Intune, having the latest OS version, or being free from security threats.

- **Location**: Restricts access based on geographical location, allowing only connections from approved regions.

- **Application**: Applies specific policies to certain apps, such as requiring multi-factor authentication (MFA) for sensitive applications like Outlook or Teams.

By creating Conditional Access policies, IT administrators can enforce security controls dynamically, adapting access permissions based on context. For iOS devices, this means that employees using mobile devices to access company resources must meet all specified security requirements, helping reduce the risk of unauthorized access.

When a user tries to access a resource, Conditional Access policies evaluate the context of the request, such as the user's identity, device state, and location, to determine if access should be allowed. Here's a breakdown of the Conditional Access workflow:

1. **User Sign-In**: The user attempts to sign in to a corporate resource, such as Microsoft Teams, Outlook, or SharePoint.

2. **Policy Evaluation**: Azure AD checks Conditional Access policies associated with the resource and evaluates the request based on predefined criteria (e.g., user identity, device compliance, and location).

3. **Grant or Deny Access**: Based on the evaluation, Conditional Access either grants access, prompts the user for additional verification (such as MFA), or denies access if the conditions aren't met.

For example, if a Conditional Access policy requires that devices accessing corporate email must be compliant with Intune policies, any non-compliant device will be denied access until it meets the necessary criteria. This protects corporate data by ensuring that only secure, authorized devices are able to access critical resources.

When setting up Conditional Access policies for iOS devices, there are several key conditions to consider that help ensure a secure mobile environment:

- **Device Compliance**: One of the most essential conditions for iOS security, this setting requires devices to meet Intune compliance policies before accessing corporate resources. This may include ensuring devices have passcode protection, encryption, and the latest OS version.

- **Location-Based Access Control**: Restrict access based on location to mitigate risk. For example, you can block sign-ins from countries where your organization doesn't operate, or only allow access from certain geographic regions.

- **Multi-Factor Authentication (MFA)**: Enforce MFA for high-risk applications, such as those handling sensitive data. This adds an additional layer of security, requiring users to confirm their identity with another method (like a phone or email code) even after entering their password.

- **Session Management**: Control how long users can stay signed in without re-authenticating. Shorter session times are ideal for apps that handle sensitive data, while longer sessions may be acceptable for low-risk resources.

These conditions allow for precise, context-based access management, ensuring that only authorized, secure devices can access corporate resources.

Implementing Conditional Access for iOS devices provides multiple layers of security and compliance benefits:

- **Enhanced Data Protection**: By requiring compliance with device security standards, Conditional Access reduces the risk of unauthorized access to corporate data, especially on mobile devices that may be used outside secure networks.

- **Reduced Risk of Data Breaches**: Conditional Access policies minimize the chances of compromised devices accessing sensitive information, protecting the organization from potential data breaches.

- **Increased Compliance**: For organizations that must adhere to strict regulations (such as GDPR or HIPAA), Conditional Access policies can help demonstrate compliance by enforcing stringent access controls.

- **Improved User Experience**: While Conditional Access enforces strict security requirements, it does so in a seamless way that doesn't disrupt users who are compliant. MFA, for example, can be triggered only when additional verification is needed, striking a balance between security and convenience.

By implementing Conditional Access, organizations gain stronger control over who and what can access sensitive data, providing a scalable solution that adapts to modern security challenges.

Setting up effective Conditional Access policies involves a strategic approach that balances security needs with user experience. Here are some best practices for creating Conditional Access policies for iOS devices:

1. **Start with Key Applications**: Begin by applying Conditional Access to critical applications, such as Outlook, Teams, and SharePoint, to secure the highest-value resources first.

2. **Use a Gradual Rollout**: Introduce Conditional Access policies gradually, testing with small groups before organization-wide deployment. This helps identify potential issues and refine policies based on feedback.

3. **Enforce Compliance Requirements**: Combine Conditional Access with device compliance policies to ensure that only devices meeting security standards can access resources. Compliance requirements should include passcodes, encryption, and OS updates.

4. **Enable Multi-Factor Authentication for High-Risk Scenarios**: Apply MFA for specific situations, such as accessing sensitive applications or signing in from an untrusted network. MFA is one of the simplest yet most effective ways to prevent unauthorized access.

5. **Review and Adjust Policies Regularly**: Periodically review Conditional Access policies to ensure they align with evolving security needs. Update policies to address new risks or changes in organizational requirements.

By following these best practices, IT can create Conditional Access policies that are effective, user-friendly, and tailored to the specific security needs of iOS devices in a corporate setting.

Conditional Access is essential for securing iOS devices, allowing organizations to implement dynamic, context-based security that adapts to modern threats. As iOS devices often operate outside secure office networks, Conditional Access policies help protect sensitive resources by enforcing strict requirements for device compliance, user verification, and secure connections.

With Conditional Access, organizations have a powerful tool for balancing accessibility with security. By configuring precise access controls, IT can safeguard corporate data while supporting a flexible, mobile workforce.

App Protection Policies for Securing Data within Apps

While Conditional Access secures who can access corporate resources, App Protection Policies (APP) add an extra layer by controlling what users can do with corporate data within specific applications. App protection policies focus on data within individual apps, protecting sensitive information even on devices that may not be fully managed by the organization. This approach is particularly valuable in BYOD (Bring Your Own Device) scenarios, where employees use their personal devices for work, as it enables IT to secure corporate data without intruding on personal content.

App protection policies in Intune are rules that control how corporate data is accessed, shared, and stored within managed apps. These policies apply directly to the app, rather than the device itself, and can be used to enforce security measures such as data encryption, access restrictions, and conditional data wipe. By focusing on the app level, APP ensures that corporate data remains secure, even on personal or unmanaged devices, without affecting personal files and apps.

App protection policies are especially useful for popular productivity apps like Outlook, OneDrive, Teams, and other Office applications, where employees handle sensitive corporate data daily.

App protection policies offer a range of security settings that allow IT administrators to define how corporate data is used and protected within managed apps. Here are some of the key settings:

- **Data Transfer Controls**: Restrict data sharing between managed (work) and unmanaged (personal) apps. For example, users can be prevented from copying text or sharing files from a corporate app to a personal app like WhatsApp or Messenger, minimizing data leaks.

- **Data Encryption**: Require encryption for all corporate data within managed apps. This setting ensures that data is securely stored, making it unreadable if accessed without authorization, which is crucial if a device is lost or stolen.

- **Access Requirements**: Define access requirements for managed apps, such as requiring users to authenticate with a PIN, password, or biometric verification (e.g., Face ID or Touch ID) before they can access corporate data. This helps prevent unauthorized access, especially if the device is shared or unlocked.

- **Conditional Data Wipe**: Configure automatic data wipe conditions for apps. This feature allows corporate data to be wiped from an app if certain conditions are met, such as a specified period of inactivity or repeated failed login attempts. This is a protective measure to ensure that data cannot be accessed if the device is compromised or falls into the wrong hands.

These settings provide IT with granular control over how corporate data is handled, adding a strong layer of security within individual apps.

App protection policies can be applied to both fully managed iOS devices and BYOD scenarios. Here's how they work in each case:

1. **Fully Managed Devices**: On fully managed devices, APP reinforces security by adding specific protections around corporate apps, creating a controlled environment where both the device and the app-level data are secured. In this case, IT has full control over both the device and the apps, allowing them to enforce comprehensive security policies.

2. **BYOD Devices**: In BYOD scenarios, APP allows IT to secure corporate data within apps on personal devices, without imposing controls over the entire device. By applying policies at the app level, users can keep personal data separate from work data. This protects their privacy while enabling IT to enforce security standards on work-related data and apps.

This flexibility makes app protection policies ideal for a mobile, modern workforce, allowing organizations to maintain data security on both corporate and personal devices.

Configuring app protection policies in Intune is straightforward and allows IT to tailor settings based on organizational needs. Here's how to set up a basic app protection policy for iOS devices:

1. **Access App Protection Policies**: In the Microsoft Endpoint Manager Admin Center, navigate to Apps > App protection policies.

2. **Create Policy**: Click **Create Policy** and select iOS/iPadOS as the platform to create a new app protection policy for iOS devices.

3. **Name and Target the Policy**: Enter a policy name and description. In the Targeted apps section, choose the apps you want the policy to protect. Commonly targeted apps include Outlook, Teams, OneDrive, and Word.

4. **Configure Data Protection Settings**:

o **Restrict Save-As**: Prevent users from saving copies of corporate documents to personal or unmanaged locations.

o **Encrypt App Data**: Enable data encryption to protect stored corporate data within the app.

o **Limit Data Transfer**: Configure settings to prevent data from being copied or transferred to unmanaged apps or storage locations.

5. **Set Access Requirements**: Define access requirements such as requiring a PIN, Face ID, or Touch ID for accessing managed apps. These requirements add an extra layer of security to prevent unauthorized access.

6. **Configure Conditional Data Wipe**: Set conditions under which app data should be automatically wiped, such as if a device is inactive for a certain number of days or if too many failed login attempts occur.

7. **Assign the Policy to User Groups**: Finally, assign the policy to relevant user groups. For instance, you might assign it to "All Corporate iOS Devices" or specific departments that require enhanced data protection.

By following these steps, you can configure a robust app protection policy that secures corporate data within essential apps, protecting it from unauthorized access or accidental leaks.

To get the most out of app protection policies, consider the following best practices:

- **Apply Policies to High-Risk Apps First**: Start with apps that handle the most sensitive data, such as email (Outlook), file storage (OneDrive), and collaboration tools (Teams). This approach ensures that critical data is protected from the start.

- **Educate Users on Policy Requirements**: Explain to users how app protection policies work and why they are important.

Understanding the policies helps users comply more easily and reduces confusion around restrictions like limited data sharing.

- **Regularly Review and Update Policies**: Security needs evolve over time, so periodically review and adjust app protection policies to align with current organizational requirements. Updating policies helps address new risks and ensure ongoing data protection.

- **Combine with Conditional Access for Enhanced Security**: App protection policies work well in tandem with Conditional Access policies, which control who can access corporate apps based on device compliance. This layered approach further strengthens security by ensuring that only compliant devices can access protected apps.

By applying these best practices, IT can maximize the effectiveness of app protection policies, safeguarding corporate data while providing a seamless user experience.

App protection policies are a critical tool for protecting corporate data within specific applications. By securing data at the app level, APP allows organizations to enforce data protection on both corporate-owned and personal devices, creating a secure yet flexible environment that adapts to diverse device ownership models. This approach is particularly valuable for BYOD scenarios, where app protection policies allow IT to secure work data on personal devices without compromising user privacy.

Together with Conditional Access, app protection policies create a comprehensive security framework that ensures sensitive data is always protected, whether it's accessed on a corporate device, a personal phone, or an unmanaged iPad.

Defining Password Policies, Encryption Requirements, and More

Compliance policies in Intune help ensure that iOS devices meet baseline security requirements before they are granted access to corporate resources. By enforcing standards such as password protection, encryption, and device health checks, IT administrators can create a secure environment that protects sensitive data from unauthorized access and minimizes security risks. Setting compliance standards is essential in maintaining a consistent level of security across all devices, particularly in a diverse mobile environment where both corporate-owned and BYOD devices may be accessing resources.

Compliance policies in Intune are rules that define the security requirements a device must meet to access corporate resources. These policies evaluate each device based on specific criteria—such as having a password, enabling encryption, or running the latest OS version—and classify it as compliant or non-compliant. Non-compliant devices can be restricted from accessing corporate resources, helping to protect data from devices that may be compromised or do not meet security standards.

For iOS devices, compliance policies focus on several core areas, including access control, data protection, and device health, ensuring that every device adheres to the same security baseline.

To secure iOS devices effectively, Intune provides a range of compliance settings that IT administrators can customize to meet organizational needs. Here are some of the most important standards to consider when setting compliance policies:

1. **Password Policies**

Password policies are essential for protecting devices from unauthorized access. Intune allows IT to define specific password requirements, such as:

- **Minimum Password Length**: Set the minimum number of characters required for a device password (e.g., six characters) to prevent weak passwords.

- **Complexity Requirements**: Require users to include alphanumeric characters or special characters to make passwords harder to guess.

- **Maximum PIN Attempts**: Define the number of failed login attempts allowed before the device is locked, reducing the risk of brute force attacks.

- **Biometric Authentication**: Enable Face ID or Touch ID for a convenient yet secure authentication method. This ensures that only the authorized user can unlock the device, adding a layer of protection beyond the standard password.

Password policies ensure that users follow best practices in creating secure passwords, minimizing the risk of unauthorized access to corporate data.

2. Encryption Requirements

Data encryption is critical for protecting information stored on a device. When encryption is enabled, data is converted into a secure format that can only be accessed by authorized users. For iOS devices, encryption is typically enabled by default, but compliance policies can be used to verify that encryption remains active and unmodified.

- **Require Device Encryption**: Enforce that all devices accessing corporate resources have encryption enabled. This setting protects sensitive data even if the device is lost or stolen, as encrypted data is inaccessible without the correct password or biometric authentication.

By ensuring encryption is active, IT can prevent unauthorized individuals from accessing corporate data stored on devices, reducing the impact of potential security incidents.

3. **Device Health Checks**

Device health checks ensure that devices meet specific security conditions, such as running an approved OS version, being free from known vulnerabilities, and avoiding jailbreaking.

- o **Operating System Version**: Specify a minimum OS version to ensure devices have the latest security patches and features. This minimizes vulnerabilities associated with outdated software.

- o **Jailbreak Detection**: Block access from jailbroken devices, as they bypass Apple's built-in security protections and are more susceptible to malware and unauthorized access.

- o **Security Patch Level**: Require devices to be up-to-date with the latest security patches, ensuring that known vulnerabilities are addressed promptly.

These health checks maintain a secure baseline across all devices, reducing the chances of security breaches due to outdated or compromised devices.

4. **Data Protection Settings**

Data protection settings focus on safeguarding corporate information within the device by controlling how data is stored and shared.

- o **Prevent Data Backup to Unmanaged Locations**: Block data backup to non-corporate storage, such as iCloud or other third-party services, ensuring that corporate data remains within managed environments.

- o **Restrict Save-As Options**: Prevent users from saving work files to personal or unmanaged locations, helping contain sensitive data within approved apps.

These data protection measures enhance data security by preventing corporate information from being stored or transferred to unapproved locations.

To set up compliance policies in Intune for iOS devices, follow these steps:

1. **Navigate to Compliance Policies**: In the Microsoft Endpoint Manager Admin Center, go to Devices > iOS/iPadOS > Compliance Policies.

2. **Create New Policy**: Select **Create Policy** and choose iOS/iPadOS as the platform.

3. **Define Compliance Settings**: Configure each compliance setting based on organizational standards:

   o Under Password, set minimum length, complexity, and maximum failed attempts.

   o In Encryption, ensure that device encryption is required.

   o Set Device Health options for OS version, jailbreak detection, and security patches.

   o Add Data Protection settings to restrict data backups and save locations.

4. **Assign the Policy to User Groups**: Assign the policy to relevant groups, such as "All Corporate iOS Devices" or department-specific groups that may have different compliance needs.

5. **Set Non-Compliance Actions**: Configure actions for non-compliance, such as notifying the user, restricting access, or requiring a remediation action (e.g., updating the OS). Non-compliance actions enforce adherence to compliance standards, helping keep devices secure.

6. **Monitor Compliance Status**: Use Intune's compliance reports to track device compliance status and review which devices are meeting or failing the established requirements. Monitoring helps ensure that policies are effective and provides insights into potential security risks.

By following these steps, IT administrators can enforce security standards that align with organizational policies, keeping iOS devices secure and compliant.

Creating effective compliance policies requires careful consideration of both security needs and user experience. Here are some best practices for implementing compliance standards in Intune:

- **Start with Core Requirements**: Focus on essential compliance settings, such as password policies, encryption, and OS version checks. Once these basics are in place, expand policies as needed.

- **Educate Users on Compliance**: Inform users of compliance requirements, such as password standards and OS update policies. Educated users are more likely to comply and understand the importance of these measures.

- **Regularly Review and Update Policies**: Periodically review compliance policies to ensure they meet current security needs. Update policies as new threats emerge or as your organization's security posture evolves.

- **Set Non-Compliance Actions Carefully**: Configure non-compliance actions that balance security with usability. For example, sending a notification allows users to remediate issues before facing access restrictions.

Implementing these best practices ensures that compliance standards are effective, adaptable, and user-friendly, contributing to a secure mobile environment.

Setting compliance standards is essential for maintaining a secure, compliant mobile environment. By enforcing password policies, encryption, and device health checks, Intune's compliance policies help protect sensitive corporate data from unauthorized access and reduce the risk of data breaches. Compliance standards also ensure that all iOS devices accessing corporate resources are equipped with the latest security protections, supporting a consistent level of security across the organization.

With these compliance policies in place, organizations can trust that their iOS devices meet security requirements, even in a diverse device landscape. This strengthens the overall security posture, making it easier to safeguard data in today's mobile-driven world.

Handling Jailbroken Devices

Jailbreaking removes the inherent security restrictions Apple places on iOS devices, allowing unauthorized access to the system and enabling unapproved applications and modifications. While this may appeal to some users for customization, it opens the device to significant security risks, such as malware, unauthorized data access, and weakened encryption. For organizations that handle sensitive data, jailbroken devices pose a serious security risk and should be treated as non-compliant.

Intune's compliance policies allow IT administrators to identify jailbroken devices and set up automatic responses to manage or restrict access, ensuring that only secure, compliant devices can access corporate resources.

When a device is jailbroken, it bypasses Apple's built-in security controls, making it more susceptible to threats such as:

- **Malware and Viruses**: Jailbroken devices can install apps from unofficial sources, increasing the likelihood of downloading malicious software.

- **Unauthorized Data Access**: Without Apple's security controls, apps can access sensitive data and interact with system files, putting corporate information at risk.

- **Privacy and Compliance Risks**: Jailbroken devices are vulnerable to data leaks, which can compromise an organization's privacy and regulatory compliance efforts.

Intune offers built-in tools to detect and flag jailbroken devices. By setting up compliance policies to check device status, Intune can identify jailbroken devices and classify them as non-compliant.

1. **Navigate to Compliance Policies**: In the Microsoft Endpoint Manager Admin Center, go to Devices > iOS/iPadOS > Compliance Policies.

2. **Create or Edit a Compliance Policy**: Select Create Policy or edit an existing policy for iOS. In the Device Health section, enable Block Jailbroken Devices.

3. **Define Non-Compliance Actions**: Set up automatic responses for non-compliance, such as notifying the user or restricting access to corporate resources.

By configuring this setting, Intune can automatically detect and classify any jailbroken devices as non-compliant, triggering the configured non-compliance actions.

Once a device is flagged as non-compliant due to jailbreaking, Intune provides several automatic actions to address the issue. Here's how to configure these responses:

1. **Notify the User**: Sending a notification to the user is a helpful first step, informing them of the non-compliance and providing instructions on how to remediate the issue. This could include guidance on restoring the device to a compliant state or contacting IT for support.

   o **Example Message**: "Your device has been identified as jailbroken and does not meet our security requirements. Please restore your device to its original configuration or contact IT for assistance."

2. **Restrict Access to Corporate Resources**: For more secure environments, you can configure Intune to restrict access to corporate applications, such as Outlook, Teams, and SharePoint, on non-compliant devices. This action prevents jailbroken

devices from accessing sensitive information until they are restored to compliance.

- o **Conditional Access Policies**: Use Conditional Access to enforce access restrictions. For example, set up a policy that blocks access to corporate resources if a device is flagged as non-compliant.

3. **Initiate a Selective Wipe**: If the device continues to remain non-compliant or poses a significant security threat, Intune allows IT to initiate a selective wipe, removing all corporate data from the device without affecting personal information.

- o **How to Set Up**: In the non-compliance action settings, select Wipe Corporate Data. This action ensures that sensitive corporate data is removed from the device if it cannot be secured.

4. **Require Device Remediation**: Some organizations may choose to set up policies that require the user to restore the device to its non-jailbroken state to regain access. This action can be combined with user notifications to provide instructions on how to return the device to compliance.

Each of these responses provides a scalable way to handle non-compliant devices, ensuring that sensitive data remains secure even if a device is jailbroken.

To effectively manage the risks associated with jailbroken devices, follow these best practices when configuring non-compliance actions:

- **Use Conditional Access Policies for Immediate Security**: By integrating Conditional Access with compliance policies, IT can automatically block jailbroken devices from accessing corporate resources. This layered approach provides real-time protection, ensuring that only compliant devices can connect to sensitive data.

- **Educate Users on Compliance Requirements**: Provide clear information about the security risks of jailbreaking and how it affects their ability to access corporate resources. An informed user is less likely to bypass security measures, and understanding the policies can reduce frustration if access is restricted.

- **Review and Update Policies Regularly**: As security threats evolve, regularly review your compliance policies and non-compliance actions to ensure they address the latest risks associated with jailbroken devices.

- **Enable Reporting and Monitoring for Compliance**: Use Intune's reporting tools to monitor compliance status across devices. Reviewing reports on non-compliant devices helps IT teams understand trends and address recurring issues proactively.

By following these practices, IT administrators can maintain control over device security while minimizing disruptions for users.

Automatically responding to jailbroken devices is a vital part of maintaining data security and compliance in a mobile environment. By setting up detection and response measures, Intune helps IT teams quickly address the risk of jailbroken devices, ensuring that only secure, compliant devices can access corporate resources. These automatic responses allow for scalable security management that keeps data protected, even in environments where BYOD policies are in place.

Together with compliance policies, Conditional Access, and app protection policies, managing jailbroken devices creates a comprehensive security framework that protects data integrity, supports compliance, and reinforces trust in the organization's mobile ecosystem.

The Compliance Conundrum

Alex leaned back in his chair, staring at his screen. Today's task was to tackle compliance policies—specifically, how to handle jailbroken devices that could jeopardize the security of corporate data. He knew that jailbroken devices posed a risk by bypassing Apple's built-in protections, and he was determined to figure out how to keep them from accessing sensitive information.

As he reviewed the settings in Intune, Alex was struck by how much control these compliance policies offered. He could actually configure Intune to detect if a device was jailbroken and, even better, set up automated responses. This was a game-changer. Instead of manually monitoring devices, Intune would handle the heavy lifting, keeping tabs on compliance and kicking in the right action if a device didn't meet security standards.

The first step was to set up a policy to detect jailbroken devices. Alex navigated through the compliance policy settings, activating the "Block Jailbroken Devices" option under Device Health. He smiled as he imagined Intune quietly working in the background, flagging any device that bypassed Apple's restrictions. This way, the system would catch potential security risks before they even became a problem.

Next, Alex turned his attention to the non-compliance actions. He knew that simply identifying jailbroken devices wasn't enough; he needed a clear plan for what would happen next. He set up an immediate user notification as the first action, drafting a message that would alert the user of their non-compliant status. His message was direct yet helpful: *"Your device has been identified as jailbroken and does not meet our security requirements. Please restore it to its original configuration or contact IT for assistance."*

With the notification in place, he took things a step further by setting up Conditional Access policies. Now, if a device was flagged as non-compliant, it would be automatically restricted from accessing key corporate resources like Outlook, Teams, and SharePoint. Alex imagined the user's experience: if they tried to access work email or files, they'd see a message explaining the access restrictions and reminding them to restore their device to compliance. It was a balance of security and guidance—just what he was aiming for.

The last action was more drastic but necessary as a final safeguard: a selective wipe. If a jailbroken device posed an immediate security threat or remained non-compliant, Intune would remove all corporate data from the device without affecting personal files. Alex appreciated how this action gave IT a way to secure sensitive information without intruding on personal content. It was a powerful solution for BYOD, where devices often had a mix of personal and work data.

As Alex set up the selective wipe, he thought about the trust his organization placed in him and the Intune policies he was building. These policies weren't just about following protocol; they were about creating a secure yet user-friendly experience. He imagined the scenarios these policies would prevent: a lost device with sensitive information, an unauthorized user trying to access files, or a device with a virus from an unapproved app. Each one was a risk he could now control, quietly and automatically.

With his policies in place, Alex ran a few tests to see how Intune would respond to a non-compliant device. He simulated a jailbroken device and watched as Intune flagged it, sent the notification, and restricted access, just as he'd configured. Everything worked seamlessly, reinforcing his confidence in the system.

By the end of the day, Alex felt accomplished. Setting up automated compliance actions wasn't just about tech—it was about foresight, protection, and empowering users to stay secure. He saw his role as more than just enforcing rules; he was helping create a safer, smarter environment where users could work without constant worry.

Tomorrow, he'd dive into the next task. But for now, he was content, knowing that each jailbroken device caught and each non-compliant alert sent would strengthen his company's security one step at a time.

As Alex moves forward, will his compliance policies hold up against real-world scenarios?

Summary and Reflection

So far, we explored the essential security and compliance policies needed to protect corporate data on iOS devices in a mobile environment. We started with Conditional Access, which helps control who can access resources by assessing factors like device compliance, user location, and app-specific policies. Conditional Access provides the first line of defense, allowing only authorized, secure devices to connect to corporate data.

Next, we delved into App Protection Policies (APP), which protect data within specific apps, even on personal devices. By enforcing policies at the app level, IT can secure work-related data without affecting users' personal information, ensuring that critical information remains contained within approved applications. APP is especially valuable in BYOD scenarios, allowing organizations to strike a balance between security and user privacy.

We then covered Setting Compliance Standards, focusing on defining policies around password requirements, encryption, and device health checks. These compliance standards create a security baseline for iOS devices, ensuring that each device meets minimum security requirements before accessing corporate resources. By requiring encryption, passwords, and the latest OS updates, these policies reinforce a secure environment.

Finally, we addressed Handling Jailbroken Devices, which pose a unique security risk. Through Intune, IT can detect jailbroken devices and automatically respond with actions like notifying the user, restricting access, or initiating a selective wipe of corporate data. This automation ensures that non-compliant devices don't compromise security.

Together, these security and compliance measures form a comprehensive framework that protects sensitive data, supports regulatory requirements, and promotes a secure mobile workspace.

In this chapter, we followed Alex as he configured various security policies to protect corporate data on iOS devices. Alex learned that maintaining security isn't just about enforcing strict access—it's about creating a layered approach that covers everything from device compliance to data protection within apps. By implementing Conditional Access, Alex could ensure that only secure, compliant devices accessed sensitive resources, while App Protection Policies allowed him to secure data within apps on both corporate and personal devices.

As he moved on to setting compliance standards, Alex saw the importance of establishing a security baseline, creating a consistent level of protection across all iOS devices. From passwords to encryption, these standards were fundamental to securing data on every device accessing company resources. Handling jailbroken devices added another layer of responsibility, with Alex learning to configure Intune to automatically detect and respond to these high-risk devices.

For Alex—and likely for you—this chapter highlights the importance of a proactive approach to security. Each policy represents a piece of a larger security strategy that protects the organization, its data, and its users. Like Alex, you're developing an understanding of how these policies interlock to create a secure, compliant environment.

Troubleshooting and Monitoring iOS Devices in Intune

Enrollment Failures, App Issues, and Policy Conflicts

Even with a well-planned deployment, issues can arise when managing iOS devices in Intune. From enrollment failures to app-related issues and policy conflicts, troubleshooting these problems is essential to ensure a smooth user experience and maintain security standards.

Enrollment is the first step in bringing a device into the Intune-managed environment, so when enrollment fails, users can't access corporate resources or policies. Here are some common enrollment issues and their solutions:

1. **User Authentication Issues**: Often, enrollment failures are related to authentication problems, such as incorrect credentials or expired passwords.

   o **Solution**: Verify the user's credentials and check that the user account is active and in good standing in Azure AD. Ensure that the user has the necessary licenses for Intune and that MFA requirements are being met, as Conditional Access policies may require MFA for enrollment.

2. **Device Limit Exceeded**: By default, users can only enroll a limited number of devices, which can cause issues if they exceed this number.

   o **Solution**: In the Intune Admin Center, go to Devices > Enrollment restrictions and review the device enrollment limit. Consider increasing the limit or advising users to unenroll old devices they no longer use.

3. **Unsupported OS Version**: Intune may have minimum OS version requirements that an outdated device does not meet.

   o **Solution**: Check the OS version requirements in the Intune compliance policies and ensure the device is running a supported version. If not, advise the user to update their device's operating system.

4. **Network Connectivity Issues**: Enrollment requires a stable internet connection. Poor connectivity can disrupt the enrollment process, causing timeouts or failures.

   o **Solution**: Advise users to connect to a stable WiFi network and try enrolling again. For mobile data connections, consider testing in a different location with better signal strength.

5. **Device Already Enrolled**: If a device has been previously enrolled with a different account, it may fail to enroll with a new account.

   o **Solution**: Perform a device reset to remove the previous enrollment settings. For BYOD users, instruct them to fully remove the old account in Settings > General > Profiles & Device Management before re-enrolling.

App-related issues can disrupt productivity and cause frustration for users. Here are common app issues and their resolutions:

1. **App Installation Failures**: When users can't install required or available apps, it may be due to device restrictions, network problems, or Intune policy configurations.

   o **Solution**: Check the app's installation status in the Intune Admin Center under Apps > App installation status. If the app failed to install, review any error codes or messages and verify that device restrictions allow app installations from the App Store.

2. **App Not Showing in Company Portal**: Users may not see assigned apps in the Company Portal if the app hasn't been assigned correctly or the user group hasn't been included in the assignment.

   o **Solution**: Confirm that the app is assigned to the correct user group. Navigate to Apps > Assignments and ensure the app assignment includes the target group. Refresh the Company Portal on the user's device by pulling down the screen to refresh.

3. **App Crashes or Poor Performance**: Sometimes, apps may crash or run poorly, often due to compatibility issues with the iOS version.

   o **Solution**: Check if there's a known compatibility issue between the app and the latest iOS update. Ensure that the app is up-to-date in the App Store, and if the issue persists, consider reinstalling the app or checking with the app vendor for compatibility fixes.

4. **Authentication Errors in Apps**: For Microsoft apps that require authentication, users may encounter login errors if the app doesn't recognize their credentials.

   o **Solution**: Ask users to log out of the app, clear the app cache, and log back in. Ensure that the app uses the same account credentials as the device's enrollment account. Additionally, check any Conditional Access policies in place, as they may require MFA or other conditions for access.

Policy conflicts can occur when multiple configurations apply to the same device or user, causing settings to override each other or apply inconsistently. Here are common policy conflicts and solutions:

1. **Conflicting Configuration Profiles**: Different configuration profiles, such as WiFi settings or email profiles, may conflict if they set contradictory values.

- o **Solution**: In the Intune Admin Center, go to Devices > Configuration profiles and review the profiles assigned to the user or device. If conflicts exist, consider consolidating profiles or removing redundant ones. When possible, limit the number of overlapping profiles to prevent conflict.

2. **Compliance vs. Conditional Access Conflicts**: Sometimes, compliance policies and Conditional Access policies can contradict each other, especially if compliance requires one condition but Conditional Access requires another.

   - o **Solution**: Review the settings in both Compliance policies and Conditional Access policies to ensure they are aligned. For example, if one policy requires a password but another blocks non-compliant devices, ensure that devices have a password before applying the Conditional Access policy.

3. **App Protection and Device Compliance Conflicts**: If App Protection Policies (APP) require settings that conflict with device compliance requirements, users may face issues accessing data within apps.

   - o **Solution**: Review the APP and device compliance settings to ensure they don't impose contradictory requirements. Align settings, such as requiring encryption or a passcode, across policies for a consistent user experience.

4. **Overlapping App Assignments**: Assigning the same app as both required and available can cause the device to receive mixed instructions, leading to unpredictable behavior.

   - o **Solution**: Check app assignment configurations and ensure that apps are either required or available for specific groups but not both. Clear, non-overlapping assignments help prevent installation issues and conflicting instructions.

While resolving issues is essential, preventing them is even better. Here are some best practices to minimize the occurrence of common issues:

- **Test Policies with a Pilot Group**: Before rolling out new policies organization-wide, test them with a pilot group to identify potential conflicts and issues. This allows IT to adjust settings before full deployment.

- **Educate Users on Best Practices**: Inform users of common issues, like needing to update their OS or checking the Company Portal for available apps. Empowered users are less likely to encounter avoidable issues.

- **Use Intune Reporting and Monitoring**: Regularly check Intune's reporting tools for enrollment status, app installation issues, and policy conflicts. Early detection helps IT address issues before they impact productivity.

- **Standardize Policy Configurations**: Avoid creating too many overlapping policies. Simplify configurations where possible to reduce policy conflicts and make troubleshooting easier.

Managing iOS devices with Intune requires a proactive approach to troubleshooting. By understanding common issues and setting up practical solutions, IT teams can ensure a smooth user experience, maintain device compliance, and support productivity. Troubleshooting isn't just about resolving issues; it's about creating an environment where users can work without frequent disruptions, while IT maintains control over security and compliance.

Using Intune's Reporting Tools

Intune's reporting tools offer valuable insights that help IT administrators monitor and maintain a healthy, compliant, and secure fleet of iOS devices. By leveraging Intune's dashboards, IT can proactively track device health, identify compliance issues, and troubleshoot problems before they disrupt user productivity. Intune's reporting features are essential for efficient device management, providing real-time visibility and actionable data.

The Intune Admin Center is the central hub for all reporting, allowing IT administrators to access an overview of device health, compliance, app status, and more. To get started, go to the Microsoft Endpoint Manager Admin Center and navigate to Reports. Here, you'll find a variety of reporting options that provide different insights into device and user activity. There are reports related to device compliance, device configuration and device attestation.

These reports make it easy to monitor overall health and quickly drill down into specific areas for further investigation. Device health monitoring helps IT keep tabs on device performance and security status, ensuring that the entire device fleet is in optimal condition.

Compliance reports in Intune allow IT administrators to track and enforce device compliance with organizational policies, ensuring that each device meets security requirements before accessing corporate resources.

1. **Compliance Overview**: Navigate to Reports > Device compliance to view a summary of compliance status across all devices. This report displays the number of compliant, non-compliant, and not evaluated devices, giving a clear picture of your overall compliance posture.

2. **Policy-Specific Compliance**: If you need to investigate specific compliance policies, Intune provides detailed reports for each policy. For example, you can review the compliance status for password policies, encryption requirements, or device health checks.

   o **Filter by Policy**: Filter the report by policy type to quickly identify which devices are failing a particular compliance standard. This helps IT teams focus on specific compliance gaps and address them more efficiently.

3. **Non-Compliance Actions**: From the compliance dashboard, IT can set up non-compliance actions such as sending notifications or restricting access. These actions help enforce compliance by alerting users of issues or temporarily blocking access to corporate resources until compliance is restored.

Compliance reporting allows IT to maintain high security standards and quickly address compliance issues across devices, keeping corporate data secure.

Tracking the status and usage of apps deployed on iOS devices helps IT ensure that users have the tools they need while identifying any installation issues or usage patterns.

1. **App Installation Status**: In the Apps section of the Intune Admin Center, go to Apps > Monitor > App installation status. This report provides an overview of app installations across all devices, showing whether apps have been installed successfully, are pending, or have failed.

   o **Troubleshoot Installations**: For failed installations, Intune provides error codes and messages, helping IT troubleshoot issues and ensure users can access their required apps.

2. **App Usage Insights**: While Intune doesn't directly track app usage frequency, it can be integrated with Microsoft 365 usage analytics for core apps like Outlook, Teams, and OneDrive. Monitoring usage data can help IT identify the most commonly used apps, assess adoption, and ensure that high-value tools are easily accessible.

   o **Optimize App Assignments**: Based on app usage insights, IT can make data-driven decisions about app deployments, adjusting assignments to better support user needs and optimize resource allocation.

By monitoring app status and usage, IT can keep critical apps up and running, identify underused apps, and enhance the overall user experience.

Intune's reporting tools are invaluable for identifying and resolving conflicts between policies, configurations, and settings. When policies overlap or conflict, they can cause unexpected behavior on devices, impacting productivity and security.

1. **Policy Conflict Report**: In the Devices section, go to Configuration profiles to monitor any policy conflicts. This report flags conflicting policies that may apply contradictory settings to the same device or user group, helping IT troubleshoot and resolve these issues before they escalate.

    o   **Resolution Tips**: Review conflicting policies and determine if they can be consolidated or if one can be prioritized over the other. Streamlining policies can reduce conflicts and improve overall device performance.

2. **Conditional Access and Compliance Conflicts**: Intune's reporting tools also identify conflicts between Conditional Access and compliance policies, which can restrict user access if not properly aligned.

    o   **Compliance vs. Conditional Access**: Ensure that Conditional Access policies don't block access based on requirements that conflict with compliance policies, such as requiring MFA or specific OS versions. Align these settings across policies to avoid unintended access restrictions.

3. **Troubleshooting Summary Dashboard**: The troubleshooting dashboard offers a quick overview of the most common issues, such as failed enrollments, app installation errors, and non-

compliance. This summary enables IT to quickly prioritize issues and address them with targeted actions.

By proactively identifying and resolving conflicts, IT can maintain consistent, predictable behavior across devices, ensuring a smoother user experience and reducing support tickets.

To maximize the effectiveness of Intune's reporting and monitoring tools, follow these best practices:

- **Set Up Regular Monitoring Routines**: Schedule regular checks on device compliance, health, and app status. Consistent monitoring allows IT to detect and resolve issues early, minimizing disruptions.

- **Automate Notifications for Critical Events**: Configure Intune to send alerts for high-priority events, such as non-compliance, app installation failures, or jailbroken devices. Real-time alerts ensure IT can respond quickly to security risks.

- **Encourage Self-Service**: Use the reporting data to create self-help resources for common issues, empowering users to troubleshoot enrollment errors or app installation problems themselves before reaching out to IT.

- **Review and Refine Policies Regularly**: Regularly review policy reports to ensure they align with your organization's current security requirements. Adjust policies to prevent conflicts and improve user experience.

These best practices help IT teams make the most of Intune's reporting tools, enabling proactive device management and efficient troubleshooting.

Intune's reporting tools are critical to a proactive device management strategy. By monitoring device health, compliance, app status, and policy conflicts, IT can anticipate issues, enforce security standards, and support user productivity. Reporting isn't just a reactive tool; it's a foundation for preventive measures that reduce downtime, maintain security, and enhance the user experience.

Remote Actions: Wiping, Locking, or Resetting a Device When Needed

In mobile device management, remote actions are essential for maintaining security and ensuring compliance. Microsoft Intune provides IT administrators with a range of remote actions, including device wiping, locking, and resetting, which allow IT to respond swiftly to lost, stolen, or non-compliant devices. These remote actions help protect corporate data, prevent unauthorized access, and restore devices to their original configuration when needed.

Intune's remote actions are powerful tools that allow IT to manage devices from anywhere. Here's an overview of the main remote actions available:

1. **Remote Wipe**: Removes all data from the device, restoring it to factory settings. This is often used when a device is lost, stolen, or permanently decommissioned.

2. **Selective Wipe**: Removes only corporate data from the device, leaving personal data intact. Ideal for BYOD scenarios where users may need to retain their personal files.

3. **Remote Lock**: Locks the device remotely, restricting access until the device is unlocked by IT or the user. Useful in cases where a device is temporarily misplaced or suspected of unauthorized use.

4. **Device Reset**: Resets the device to its default settings, erasing all data and configurations. This action is similar to a remote wipe but is generally used to prepare devices for reassignment or reconfiguration.

5. **Passcode Reset**: Resets the device passcode, allowing IT to set a new passcode if a user forgets their login credentials. This action is typically used in secure corporate environments to regain access.

A remote wipe removes all data from the device and returns it to factory settings. This action is generally used when a device is lost, stolen, or permanently decommissioned, ensuring that no corporate data remains accessible. Here's how to perform a remote wipe in Intune:

1. **Initiate the Wipe**: In the Intune Admin Center, go to Devices > All devices. Select the device you want to wipe, then choose Wipe from the available actions.

2. **Confirm the Wipe**: You'll be prompted to confirm the action, as it will permanently erase all data on the device. For lost or stolen devices, enable the option to wipe the device even if it's offline, so it will execute the wipe as soon as the device connects to the internet.

3. **Notify the User (Optional)**: For devices that aren't lost or stolen, notify the user of the wipe, explaining the reason and providing guidance on obtaining a replacement or re-enrollment if applicable.

A remote wipe is irreversible, so it should be used only when necessary. For BYOD devices, consider a selective wipe to protect the user's personal data.

In BYOD environments, a full remote wipe may be unnecessary and could disrupt personal data. A selective wipe removes only corporate data and applications, preserving the user's personal information. This action is ideal for scenarios where an employee leaves the company or if a device no longer meets compliance requirements.

1. **Initiate the Selective Wipe**: In the Intune Admin Center, go to Devices > All devices and select the device. Choose Retire or Selective wipe to initiate the action.

2. **Specify Data to Remove**: Intune will automatically remove corporate apps, email profiles, and data protected by app protection policies. The selective wipe will leave personal apps and data unaffected.

3. **Confirm with the User**: If possible, inform the user that their work data will be removed, especially if they are departing the organization. This helps maintain transparency and ensures they're aware of the data changes on their device.

Selective wipes help maintain privacy and security in BYOD setups, ensuring corporate data is removed without impacting the user's personal content.

A remote lock is a temporary measure that locks the device, preventing unauthorized access until the device is recovered or the user contacts IT. Remote locks are useful when a device is misplaced but expected to be found or if unauthorized access is suspected.

1. **Initiate the Remote Lock**: In the Intune Admin Center, go to Devices > All devices and select the device you want to lock. Choose Remote lock from the available actions.

2. **Notify the User (Optional)**: Let the user know that their device has been locked and provide instructions for unlocking it or contacting IT if needed. This helps minimize confusion and provides a direct line for assistance.

A remote lock can serve as an immediate security measure for protecting data on a misplaced device while giving the user time to retrieve it.

The device reset action restores the device to its default settings, removing all data and configurations. This action is often used when devices are reassigned to a new user or require reconfiguration.

1. **Initiate the Reset**: In the Intune Admin Center, go to Devices > All devices and select the device. Choose Reset from the available actions.

2. **Confirm the Action**: Confirm the reset action, which will clear all data and return the device to a state ready for new enrollment.

3. **Notify the User (Optional)**: Inform the original user, if applicable, that the device will be reset and reassigned, providing

instructions for re-enrollment if they will continue using it under a new setup.

A device reset is effective for reassigning devices, especially in shared device environments, as it removes all user data and configurations, preparing the device for the next user.

If a user forgets their passcode or is locked out of their device, a passcode reset allows IT to set a new passcode and restore access. This action is particularly useful in secure environments where access control is critical.

1. **Initiate the Passcode Reset**: In the Intune Admin Center, go to Devices > All devices and select the device. Choose Passcode reset from the actions menu.

2. **Set a New Passcode (if prompted)**: In some cases, you may need to set a new passcode directly or provide instructions for the user to reset it through self-service options.

3. **Notify the User**: Inform the user of the new passcode or guide them through resetting it themselves, helping them regain access quickly.

Passcode resets minimize downtime for users and help IT maintain access control over devices, ensuring quick resolution when users are locked out.

To ensure that remote actions are effective and used responsibly, follow these best practices:

- **Prioritize Selective Wipes in BYOD Environments**: To respect user privacy, use selective wipes over full wipes for BYOD devices. This maintains data security without impacting personal information.

- **Establish Clear Communication Protocols**: Notify users whenever possible before performing remote actions, especially wipes or resets. Clear communication builds trust and ensures users understand the reason for the action.

- **Limit Remote Actions to Security Incidents**: Avoid using remote actions unless necessary to address a security risk or operational need. Reserve actions like remote wipes for lost or compromised devices.

- **Document Remote Actions**: Maintain a record of all remote actions taken in Intune, including the reason for each action and the affected device. Documentation is essential for auditing and compliance purposes.

These practices help IT balance security needs with user experience, ensuring remote actions are applied responsibly and transparently.

Remote actions in Intune are critical tools for maintaining a secure, compliant mobile environment. By allowing IT to wipe, lock, or reset devices remotely, Intune enables fast, responsive action in the face of security threats, lost devices, or non-compliance. Remote actions also support privacy by allowing selective wipes in BYOD contexts, protecting corporate data without affecting personal files.

Together with real-time monitoring and alerts, remote actions provide IT with the tools needed to maintain control over devices, protect sensitive information, and ensure a smooth user experience.

The Power of Remote Actions

Alex was no stranger to troubleshooting, but today he was diving into one of Intune's most powerful features: remote actions. He understood that mobile device management wasn't just about setting up policies; it was about taking decisive action when something went wrong. And today, he was ready to learn how to lock, wipe, or reset devices as needed to keep his organization's data secure.

It started with a call from Sophie in accounting. She'd misplaced her iPad over the weekend and was frantic—she knew her device contained sensitive data, and she didn't want it to fall into the wrong hands. Alex knew that this was a perfect moment to test Intune's Remote Lock. In a few clicks, he located Sophie's device in the Intune Admin Center, selected Remote Lock, and hit confirm. Within moments, the iPad was locked, and any attempts to access it would be blocked until Sophie found it or contacted IT again.

Sophie was relieved, but Alex wasn't done yet. He talked her through what would happen next: if she didn't find her iPad by the end of the day, they'd move on to a Remote Wipe. "Don't worry," he reassured her. "We'll make sure your data stays safe, no matter what."

That same afternoon, Alex faced a different situation. This time, it was Daniel from marketing, who was transitioning out of the company. His phone was a BYOD device, and while it had been invaluable for work, it also contained a blend of personal and corporate data. Alex wanted to make sure all company information was removed without affecting Daniel's personal files. Using Selective Wipe, Alex clicked through the options to remove only the corporate data—email, files, and apps— leaving Daniel's personal content untouched.

After a quick phone call to Daniel, Alex confirmed that the corporate data had been removed successfully. Daniel still had his photos, messages, and apps intact, which reassured him as he moved on. Alex realized that selective wipes weren't just about security—they were about maintaining a level of respect for users' personal data, a key part of the balance in a BYOD environment.

Just when he thought his day couldn't get more interesting, an alert popped up for a Jailbroken Device Detected. Alex's heart skipped a beat; jailbroken devices were risky, especially since they could bypass key security protocols. The device belonged to a temporary contractor who hadn't realized the implications of jailbreaking. Alex immediately pulled up the Device Compliance settings and issued a Remote Wipe. He set it to take effect as soon as the device reconnected to the internet.

For Alex, the ability to act in real time was empowering. He knew that Intune's remote actions weren't just tools—they were the safeguards that allowed him to protect corporate data and maintain security no matter where devices were. He started to think of these actions as part of his toolkit, enabling him to react quickly to real-world problems.

As the day wound down, Alex reviewed his actions. In a single day, he had used Remote Lock to secure a misplaced device, Selective Wipe to respectfully separate corporate data from personal content, and Remote Wipe to protect data on a high-risk device. Each of these actions had a purpose, and each made him feel a little more in control.

Tomorrow, he'd be diving into Optimizing Intune Reports for Continuous Improvement, where he could analyze these actions and see how they played a part in the larger picture of security and compliance. But for now, he felt a sense of accomplishment, knowing he had the tools to keep devices secure—even from a distance.

Alex's journey with remote actions continues to illustrate the power of proactive security.

Summary and Reflection

In this chapter, we explored essential tools and strategies for managing iOS devices in Intune. From troubleshooting common issues to setting up real-time alerts and using remote actions, each feature contributes to a proactive and secure device management environment.

We began by identifying Common Issues and Resolutions for Intune deployments, covering common challenges like enrollment failures, app installation problems, and policy conflicts. Each of these issues, while common, can disrupt productivity if not addressed promptly. By understanding their causes and having solutions ready, IT administrators can minimize downtime and create a smoother experience for users.

Next, we examined Intune's Reporting Tools and their role in providing visibility into device health, compliance, and app usage. Real-time insights into compliance status, installation failures, and policy conflicts allow IT to take action early, preventing minor issues from escalating into larger problems. This approach supports not only security but also operational efficiency, as it ensures devices stay compliant and users have uninterrupted access to the tools they need.

Finally, we explored Remote Actions in Intune, focusing on wiping, locking, or resetting devices when needed. These actions empower IT to take immediate action on lost, stolen, or non-compliant devices, ensuring that corporate data remains secure regardless of the device's location. Remote actions like selective wipe, remote lock, and passcode reset offer a flexible approach, balancing security with user privacy, especially in BYOD environments.

Together, these tools enable a comprehensive approach to mobile device management, allowing IT to monitor, secure, and manage devices proactively.

We also followed Alex as he learned to troubleshoot, monitor, and remotely manage iOS devices. Alex's experience demonstrated that effective device management goes beyond configuring policies; it's about maintaining control over devices in real time. With each step—from responding to enrollment errors to remotely locking a misplaced device—Alex gained confidence in using Intune to handle challenges swiftly and maintain a secure environment.

For Alex—and likely for you—this chapter highlighted the importance of proactive, responsive device management. By using reporting tools, and knowing when to employ remote actions, Alex was able to keep his organization's mobile environment secure and responsive to users' needs. Each action, from issuing a selective wipe to resetting a passcode, reinforced his role as both a protector of data and a supporter of users.

In many ways, Alex's journey mirrors the experience of any IT administrator using Intune. With real-time monitoring, remote actions, and clear reporting, you can keep devices secure, troubleshoot issues effectively, and create a reliable experience for end users.

Best Practices and Tips

Tips for Setting Effective Policies that Aren't Overly Restrictive

When managing iOS devices in Intune, striking a balance between robust security and a seamless user experience is essential. Effective policies protect corporate data while allowing users the flexibility they need to work productively. If policies are too restrictive, users may experience frustration or find ways to bypass them, undermining security efforts. Conversely, overly lax policies can leave sensitive data vulnerable to threats. The key to success is finding a middle ground that enforces essential security standards without compromising usability.

1. Start with Essential Security Policies

Focus on core security requirements as a foundation before layering additional policies. Essential security standards include enforcing passcodes, encryption, and device compliance checks. By starting with these critical policies, you create a secure baseline that doesn't overwhelm users.

- **Example**: Require a passcode and device encryption for all devices, but avoid adding complex password requirements immediately. Once users are comfortable, more granular policies can be introduced as necessary.

2. Avoid Overlapping Policies

Overlapping policies can create confusion, conflicts, and unintended restrictions, frustrating users who may struggle with redundant or conflicting settings. Streamline policies by consolidating configurations to prevent duplicate requirements.

- **Tip**: Review all configuration and compliance policies to ensure that settings aren't duplicated across multiple profiles. For instance, if a policy enforces WiFi settings, avoid adding multiple WiFi profiles that could conflict, causing connectivity issues.

3. Consider BYOD Flexibility with Selective Policies

For BYOD users, enforce security only on corporate data and apps rather than the entire device. Selective policies allow users to access work resources securely without restricting their personal data or apps, which respects user privacy and reduces friction.

- **Selective Wipe for BYOD**: Configure app protection policies that control only work apps, like Outlook and Teams, on personal devices. This approach ensures corporate data is secure without impacting the user's personal apps or files.

4. Implement Conditional Access Carefully

Conditional Access policies are powerful tools for controlling access, but overly strict settings can frustrate users by blocking access from unexpected locations or devices. Instead of applying strict restrictions universally, tailor Conditional Access based on user roles, app sensitivity, and location.

- **Example**: Require MFA for high-risk applications or when users access resources from unfamiliar locations. This allows frequent access from trusted devices without additional prompts, preserving a smooth experience.

5. Leverage App Protection Policies for Data Security Without Device Control

App protection policies (APP) provide a lighter security layer that focuses on corporate apps and data, making them ideal for BYOD environments. APP ensures that data remains protected within managed apps without requiring device-level management, which is especially useful for users hesitant about enrolling personal devices.

- **Example**: Use APP to require encryption and prevent data transfer to unmanaged apps. For instance, block the ability to copy data from Outlook to personal apps, ensuring that corporate data stays within managed boundaries without disrupting personal activities.

6. Educate Users on Policies and Compliance

A well-informed user base is more likely to comply with security policies. Providing context about why certain security measures are in place and offering guidance on how to work within them can increase acceptance and cooperation.

- **Tip**: Offer short training sessions or documentation explaining key policies, such as the importance of compliance for accessing corporate data. Educating users reduces resistance, makes troubleshooting easier, and empowers them to work within the system effectively.

7. Regularly Review and Update Policies Based on Feedback

Gathering user feedback on existing policies helps ensure that settings remain relevant and user-friendly. Regularly review compliance and security policies, taking into account any recurring issues or complaints. Updating policies based on user experience and security trends keeps the balance between security and productivity.

- **Tip**: Set up periodic policy reviews and send user surveys to gather feedback on policies like app restrictions, password requirements, and Conditional Access. Use insights to adjust policies as needed.

8. Set Realistic Compliance Requirements

It's crucial to set compliance requirements that devices can reasonably meet. For instance, avoid requiring the latest OS version if a significant portion of devices are not yet compatible. Instead, set realistic compliance goals that align with the devices in your organization.

- **Example:** If some devices are not yet compatible with the latest iOS version, set a slightly lower OS requirement and notify users of upcoming updates. This approach prevents non-compliance issues that could block access and frustrate users.

9. Test Policies with a Pilot Group Before Full Rollout

Before deploying new policies organization-wide, test them with a small, representative group of users. Pilot testing allows you to assess the policy's impact on both security and user experience, making adjustments before full deployment if needed.

- **Tip:** Select a pilot group that includes users from various roles and departments, as different users may have unique needs. This ensures a well-rounded perspective on how the policies affect daily workflows.

10. Use Intune's Reporting Tools to Identify and Address Friction Points

Intune's reporting tools provide insights into compliance status, failed app installations, and non-compliance alerts, helping IT identify areas where users may be struggling. Analyzing these reports enables IT to address issues, refine policies, and optimize the balance between security and usability.

- **Tip:** Monitor reports for trends in compliance failures or frequent app installation issues. If certain settings consistently cause problems, consider relaxing or modifying them to better accommodate user needs.

By balancing security policies with user experience considerations, IT can create an environment where users feel empowered, not restricted. A flexible approach respects users' needs while upholding security standards, ensuring that policies are effective without being burdensome. When users feel that policies are reasonable and manageable, they're more likely to embrace them, resulting in a more secure and productive organization.

Best Practices for Keeping Devices Secure

Keeping iOS devices compliant and data secure is an ongoing responsibility that requires proactive management and a structured approach. Microsoft Intune provides tools and policies to enforce security standards, but maintaining compliance over time requires thoughtful planning, regular monitoring, and consistent user education. By implementing best practices, IT can ensure that all devices adhere to security protocols, safeguarding sensitive information and reducing the risk of breaches.

1. Implement and Regularly Update Compliance Policies

Compliance policies are the foundation of a secure mobile environment. These policies define the minimum requirements for device access, including passcode protection, encryption, and OS updates. It's essential to keep compliance policies updated in response to emerging threats and technology changes.

- **Example**: Set policies that require devices to use a passcode, enable encryption, and stay up-to-date with the latest iOS security patches. Regularly review and adjust these policies to account for new security threats or changes in OS capabilities.

2. Use Conditional Access for Real-Time Compliance Enforcement

Conditional Access allows IT to enforce compliance in real time by evaluating device health and other criteria before granting access to corporate resources. This dynamic security measure ensures that only secure and compliant devices can access sensitive data.

- **Tip**: Implement Conditional Access policies that restrict access based on compliance status. For example, block non-compliant devices from accessing critical applications like email and SharePoint until they meet the required security standards. This encourages users to keep their devices secure and compliant.

3. Enable Multi-Factor Authentication (MFA) for Added Security

Multi-Factor Authentication provides an extra layer of security, especially for high-risk applications or sensitive data access. MFA requires users to verify their identity using a second method, such as a code sent to their mobile device, reducing the risk of unauthorized access.

- **Example**: Configure MFA for applications that handle sensitive data, such as Outlook, Teams, or internal apps. Pairing MFA with Conditional Access further strengthens data security, as users must meet multiple requirements to gain access.

4. Regularly Monitor Compliance Reports and Address Non-Compliance Promptly

Intune's reporting tools provide insights into device compliance status, highlighting any non-compliant devices or areas where users may struggle with policy adherence. Regularly monitoring these reports enables IT to identify trends, address issues quickly, and ensure overall compliance.

- **Tip**: Set up regular compliance audits and use Intune's dashboards to monitor device health, compliance status, and security risks. Address non-compliance issues promptly by notifying users or enforcing non-compliance actions, like restricting access, to encourage adherence to security protocols.

5. Educate Users on Security Best Practices and Compliance Requirements

User education is essential for fostering a culture of security and ensuring compliance. When users understand why compliance policies are in place and how to follow them, they're more likely to adhere to them consistently. Provide resources that outline security best practices and the importance of compliance.

- **Tip**: Host brief security workshops or provide documentation on compliance requirements, such as how to set up secure passwords, update the OS, and recognize phishing attempts. When users know the reasons behind security protocols, they're more likely to comply voluntarily.

6. Use App Protection Policies to Control Data Within Applications

App Protection Policies (APP) offer a way to secure corporate data within specific apps, particularly useful for BYOD scenarios. By applying data protection at the app level, APP ensures that sensitive information stays protected even on devices that aren't fully managed.

- **Example**: Configure APP to enforce encryption and data transfer restrictions within corporate apps, like Outlook and Teams. Prevent users from copying corporate data to unmanaged apps or personal storage, ensuring that sensitive information remains contained.

7. Enforce Encryption on All Devices to Protect Data at Rest

Encryption is a crucial security measure that safeguards data stored on devices, making it unreadable to unauthorized users. By enforcing encryption policies in Intune, IT can protect sensitive information even if a device is lost or stolen.

- **Tip**: Set a compliance policy that requires device encryption, ensuring all data on managed devices is protected. For iOS devices, ensure that encryption is enabled by default, as it is built into iOS devices when a passcode is set.

8. Use Remote Actions for Lost or Non-Compliant Devices

Intune's remote actions—such as remote wipe, selective wipe, and lock—allow IT to take immediate action on lost, stolen, or non-compliant devices. Remote actions enable quick responses that prevent unauthorized access and help maintain data security.

- **Example**: For lost devices, initiate a remote lock to restrict access temporarily. If the device is confirmed as lost or stolen, perform a full remote wipe to ensure that all corporate data is removed, preventing data breaches.

9. Perform Regular Audits and Policy Reviews to Adapt to New Threats

The security landscape is constantly evolving, making it essential to review and update compliance policies regularly. Performing regular audits helps IT ensure that all devices meet the latest security standards and adapt policies as new threats emerge.

- **Example**: Conduct quarterly reviews of compliance and Conditional Access policies to assess their effectiveness and relevance. Adjust policies based on feedback, security trends, and any new features in Intune or iOS that enhance device security.

Maintaining compliance and data security in Intune requires a balance of proactive management, user education, and timely intervention. By implementing and regularly updating compliance policies, using Conditional Access to enforce standards, and educating users on security best practices, IT can create a secure environment that minimizes risks while supporting productivity. Remote actions and automated alerts add layers of responsiveness that allow IT to act quickly in the event of security incidents.

Ultimately, these best practices ensure that devices remain secure and compliant, protecting sensitive data and maintaining the trust of users and stakeholders.

Continuous Monitoring and Policy Adjustments

In mobile device management, setting up policies and configurations is just the beginning. Effective management requires continuous monitoring and periodic adjustments to ensure that policies stay aligned with both organizational needs and the latest security standards. As new threats emerge and user needs evolve, regularly reviewing and refining policies is essential to maintaining a secure and user-friendly environment.

Why Continuous Monitoring and Policy Adjustments Are Essential

1. **Adapt to Emerging Security Threats**: Cybersecurity threats are constantly evolving, and what may have been a robust security policy last year might be inadequate now. Regular reviews allow IT to adapt policies in response to new vulnerabilities, ensuring that devices remain protected.

2. **Support Organizational Changes**: As the organization grows, hires new employees, or adapts to new workflows, device requirements may shift. By adjusting policies to fit current needs,

IT can support a dynamic work environment without compromising security.

3. **Enhance User Experience**: Policies that were once effective might become restrictive over time. Monitoring user feedback and device performance allows IT to refine policies, making them less intrusive while maintaining compliance, which enhances user satisfaction and productivity.

4. **Optimize Policy Effectiveness**: Continuous monitoring helps IT identify policies that may not be performing as expected, such as configurations with high non-compliance rates. Regular adjustments ensure that policies are not only secure but also practical for users to follow.

How to Regularly Review and Adjust Policies in Intune

1. **Set Up a Regular Policy Review Schedule**

Establish a routine schedule for policy reviews, such as quarterly or biannually, to assess each policy's effectiveness and relevance. A structured schedule ensures that no critical policies are overlooked, and it allows IT to make timely adjustments based on any changes within the organization or the security landscape.

   o **Tip**: Use a checklist during each review cycle to assess critical areas, such as compliance policies, Conditional Access settings, app protection policies, and device configurations.

2. **Monitor Compliance Reports for Insights**

Intune's compliance reports provide insights into which devices are compliant, which are not, and why. Reviewing these reports helps IT identify patterns of non-compliance, pinpointing policies that may be too stringent or need modification to improve adherence.

o **Example**: If a significant number of devices are failing a specific compliance check, like OS version requirements, consider adjusting the policy to allow more flexibility, then gradually tighten it as users update their devices.

3. Gather User Feedback on Policies

User feedback is invaluable for identifying policies that may be causing friction. Periodically survey users, especially after implementing new policies or making significant changes, to understand how policies impact their workflow and to gather suggestions for improvement.

o **Tip**: Ask for specific feedback on settings like Conditional Access requirements, password policies, and app restrictions. This direct input can reveal practical adjustments to balance security with user experience.

4. Stay Updated on Intune and iOS Feature Updates

Microsoft and Apple frequently release updates with new features and settings for Intune and iOS. Regularly reviewing release notes allows IT to take advantage of new security configurations, management features, or optimizations, potentially reducing the need for custom configurations.

o **Example**: When Apple introduces enhanced encryption settings, consider integrating them into compliance policies to strengthen device security with minimal configuration effort.

5. Evaluate the Impact of Policy Conflicts

Policy conflicts can occur when multiple policies apply different configurations to the same device or group, leading to user frustration or unintended behavior. Regularly reviewing policies for overlapping or conflicting settings helps reduce these issues.

- o **Example**: If different configuration profiles set conflicting WiFi settings, consider consolidating them into one profile to ensure a seamless experience. Use Intune's reporting to identify and resolve any policy conflicts.

6. **Conduct Security Audits and Compliance Checks**

Security audits help verify that all devices meet baseline security requirements. Conduct audits annually or semi-annually, focusing on compliance with regulatory standards, data protection, and access control. Compliance checks validate that policies support industry and legal requirements.

- o **Tip**: Run reports to confirm that devices meet compliance standards and that access controls align with regulatory requirements like GDPR or HIPAA. If necessary, adjust policies to close any compliance gaps.

7. **Incorporate Automation for Routine Adjustments**

Automation can streamline repetitive policy adjustments, reducing the manual workload and ensuring consistency. Use Intune's automation features to deploy routine updates, enforce compliance, and adjust Conditional Access settings automatically based on predefined triggers.

- o **Example**: Configure Conditional Access policies to automatically restrict access for devices that fall out of compliance until they are restored, minimizing the need for manual intervention.

8. **Document Policy Adjustments and Rationale**

Keep detailed records of all policy changes, including the reason for adjustments, the impact on users, and any feedback that influenced the decision. This documentation creates a historical record that can guide future adjustments and help explain policy decisions if questions arise.

> o **Tip**: Store change logs in a centralized, easily accessible location, and include notes on the purpose and outcomes of each change. This documentation is valuable for audits, troubleshooting, and continuous improvement.

By continuously monitoring and adjusting policies, IT can create a more adaptable, resilient mobile device environment that aligns with both security goals and user needs. Regular policy adjustments help:

- **Maintain High Security Standards**: Ongoing updates ensure that all devices stay protected against the latest threats, keeping the organization's data secure.

- **Support Evolving User Needs**: Refining policies based on user feedback and incident data allows IT to make policies more user-friendly, improving compliance and reducing friction.

- **Enhance Operational Efficiency**: Regular adjustments reduce the number of support tickets related to policy conflicts or restrictive configurations, enabling IT to focus on proactive security measures.

Continuous monitoring and adjustments are essential to creating an effective device management strategy. By regularly reviewing policies, gathering feedback, and staying updated on new features, IT can keep security policies relevant, practical, and user-centered. As the organization grows and technology advances, these best practices ensure that Intune policies support a secure, adaptable, and productive mobile environment.

The Adjustment Game

Alex was starting to feel like he finally had a handle on Intune. He'd set up compliance policies, applied app protections, configured Conditional Access, and even mastered remote actions. But today, he faced a new challenge: ensuring his configurations remained effective over time. It was time to dive into continuous monitoring and policy adjustments, a proactive approach to keeping devices secure and users happy.

The first sign that he needed to make adjustments came during a morning review of compliance reports. Alex spotted an unusual spike in non-compliance among a group of users who couldn't meet the OS version requirement. He realized that not all devices were updating to the latest iOS as quickly as he'd hoped, especially older ones. If he kept the current policy, these users would be locked out, leading to frustration—and a flood of support tickets.

Sitting back in his chair, Alex decided to adjust the compliance policy. He tweaked the OS requirement, giving users an extra month to update before access restrictions would kick in. This way, everyone would have time to upgrade without feeling pressured or inconvenienced. The flexibility would keep users compliant and reduce any immediate disruptions. He felt a sense of relief, knowing he could solve the issue before it even became a problem.

Later that day, Alex received a call from Sarah, a sales rep who had been traveling internationally. Sarah was frustrated because her Conditional Access settings required MFA for every login attempt, and the constant verifications were slowing her down while trying to work on the go. After talking with Sarah, Alex realized that the Conditional Access policy didn't need to be quite so strict for trusted corporate apps. For apps like Outlook and Teams, he could set MFA only for sign-ins from unfamiliar locations, making it less intrusive.

With a few clicks, Alex adjusted the policy, allowing for more flexible access while still keeping security intact. He sent Sarah a quick message explaining the change, and she responded almost instantly with a thankful thumbs-up emoji. Alex felt a small rush of satisfaction—he was learning that user feedback was just as valuable as the reports he analyzed. Sometimes, a little empathy and a few adjustments were all it took to find the right balance.

As the week went on, Alex made it a point to monitor Intune's dashboards and analyze the alerts. He noticed that certain configurations, like WiFi settings, were conflicting across profiles for some devices, leading to connectivity problems. Alex consolidated the settings into a single, streamlined profile, eliminating the redundancy. After implementing the change, he observed that device connectivity issues decreased significantly, and fewer support tickets came in related to WiFi.

By the end of the week, Alex had developed a new habit. He'd start each morning with a quick check of compliance and incident reports, scanning for patterns that might indicate user frustration or potential security gaps. He made small adjustments here and there, aware now that policies weren't just "set and forget" configurations; they were living frameworks that required regular attention.

Reflecting on the week's work, Alex felt he'd discovered a new layer of Intune management. Continuous monitoring and thoughtful adjustments were what made Intune truly effective. He realized that managing policies was like tending a garden—it required care, attention, and sometimes pruning to let the system thrive.

Summary and Reflection

In this chapter, we explored strategies that help IT administrators create an effective balance between security and usability, keeping iOS devices compliant and adaptable to changing needs. These best practices focus on ensuring that security policies protect data without being overly restrictive, thus maintaining a productive environment for users.

We began with Balancing Security and User Experience, where we discussed tips for setting policies that protect data without compromising usability. This included avoiding overly restrictive configurations, using Conditional Access judiciously, and selecting policies that support both corporate and BYOD devices. The goal was to create policies that are secure yet flexible enough to meet different user needs.

Next, we looked at Maintaining Compliance and Data Security by enforcing essential security measures like multi-factor authentication, encryption, app protection policies, and using remote actions for lost or compromised devices. These practices create a secure baseline that allows IT to respond proactively to potential risks, preserving data security and ensuring compliance.

The chapter also covered Continuous Monitoring and Policy Adjustments to keep policies relevant over time. By regularly reviewing compliance reports, gathering user feedback, and adapting policies in response to new security threats or organizational changes, IT can create a responsive and resilient mobile environment. Monitoring and adjusting policies ensure that security measures remain practical and effective, supporting both the organization's security needs and user productivity.

In this chapter, Alex experienced firsthand the importance of continuous monitoring, user feedback, and thoughtful policy adjustments. He learned that effective device management isn't a one-time setup; it's an ongoing process that requires attention to detail and a willingness to adapt. Through Alex's story, we saw the impact of aligning policies with real-world needs—how even small adjustments can resolve compliance issues, improve user satisfaction, and reduce support requests.

For Alex—and for you—this chapter highlighted the need for flexibility in mobile device management. By implementing best practices like balancing security with usability, regularly updating policies, and using feedback loops, Alex was able to refine his approach, ensuring a secure yet user-friendly environment. This proactive, adaptable approach is at the core of successful device management in Intune.

Final Thoughts

Alex sat back in his chair, scrolling through his Intune dashboard one last time. The once-foreign interface now felt like home, a familiar landscape filled with policies, compliance reports, and device health metrics. He couldn't help but think back to when he first started managing iOS devices with Intune. Back then, he'd been overwhelmed by the complexity of it all—compliance policies, Conditional Access, remote actions. Each term had seemed like a barrier to understanding, and every feature felt like a mountain to climb.

But now, after months of diving into Intune's capabilities, Alex could see how each piece fit into the bigger picture. It had been quite a journey, filled with challenges, adjustments, and small victories. He'd learned that device management was more than just setting policies; it was about creating a seamless, secure experience for users while safeguarding the organization's data.

As he reflected on his journey, he realized how much he had grown—not just in technical skills, but in understanding the balance between security and usability. Intune had become a toolkit he could rely on, each feature adding a layer of control, security, or ease to his work.

In those early days, Alex had been eager to set up basic compliance policies and enforce security standards. He'd learned the importance of essentials like password policies, encryption, and compliance checks, creating a secure baseline that protected the organization's data while being simple enough for users to understand. Through trial and error, he'd learned to set realistic standards—policies that would keep devices secure without overwhelming users. This foundation gave him confidence and a sense of direction.

Then came the challenge of understanding Conditional Access and App Protection Policies. Alex quickly realized that these tools weren't just about blocking access or securing data in apps; they were about building trust. Every time he configured a policy, he was creating a balance between allowing users the freedom they needed and protecting the organization from potential threats. Conditional Access allowed him to enforce compliance dynamically, and App Protection Policies gave him control over corporate data even on personal devices. These tools empowered him to make security seamless, an experience rather than an obstacle.

Just as he was finding his rhythm, new challenges arrived. Devices went missing, users forgot passcodes, and compliance reports started to pile up. Alex quickly realized that keeping devices secure wasn't just about setting policies but also about being responsive and adaptable. He learned to use remote actions—wiping, locking, and resetting devices on the fly to ensure data security.

Each action brought a lesson: the power of immediacy in device management. Whether it was locking a device temporarily for a user who had misplaced it or issuing a selective wipe for an employee leaving the organization, these remote actions allowed him to respond swiftly and effectively. With each scenario, he felt his skills solidifying, gaining a new level of confidence in Intune's ability to handle unexpected situations.

Monitoring became second nature as well. He had set up alerts for non-compliant devices, app installation issues, and Conditional Access denials. The ability to catch issues as they happened gave Alex a proactive edge, allowing him to step in before minor problems became full-blown disruptions.

One of the biggest turning points for Alex had come when he realized that user experience mattered as much as security. He had learned to adjust policies based on feedback, finding ways to meet compliance requirements without frustrating users. This led him to his mantra: balance. By listening to users and staying open to making adjustments, he found ways to make security policies feel almost invisible—strong but not restrictive.

Alex saw firsthand the importance of continuous monitoring and regular policy adjustments. Compliance requirements that were too strict often led to user dissatisfaction, and too lenient policies left gaps in security.

By analyzing Intune's reports, gathering user feedback, and adjusting policies when needed, he found a way to create a secure yet flexible environment. Device management became less about strict rules and more about a dynamic approach that supported both security and usability.

As his skills grew, so did his desire to streamline his work. He explored Intune's automation features, discovering ways to reduce repetitive tasks, automatically enforce compliance, and respond to common issues. Automation became his ally, allowing him to handle high-priority alerts while Intune managed the routine tasks. Every automated rule he set up felt like a victory, a small way of reclaiming time and focusing on higher-level strategies.

With automation, Alex transformed his role. Tasks that used to take hours were now completed in minutes. Enrolling devices, enforcing compliance, and monitoring app installation status became a smooth process that freed up his time to focus on strategic goals. He could finally step back and see the bigger picture, knowing that Intune was doing the heavy lifting in the background.

Alex knew that this was just one part of his journey. Managing iOS devices with Intune had been his starting point, but the platform offered much more. From Android devices to complex app deployments, there was a whole world of Intune features he hadn't yet explored. As his organization continued to grow, so would the challenges—and he felt ready to take them on.

The skills he had gained in managing iOS devices would serve as the foundation for whatever came next. He had learned to be adaptable, to seek balance, and to approach security with empathy for the user experience. As he powered down his computer, Alex knew he wasn't closing the book on his Intune journey. Instead, he was preparing for the next chapter.

He thought about the colleagues and other IT administrators just starting their Intune journey. His advice to them would be simple: embrace the learning curve. Every policy, every compliance check, every troubleshooting experience would add to their understanding. And just like him, they would find their rhythm, mastering the platform one policy at a time.

As he walked away from his desk, Alex felt a sense of closure. His adventure with iOS devices had come full circle, but the doors to further growth were wide open. He'd grown from a newcomer into a confident Intune administrator, ready to face new challenges, explore deeper capabilities, and help others along the way.

Alex's journey with Intune may have started with iOS devices, but it's only the beginning. For those following in his footsteps, remember that Intune isn't just a tool—it's a platform for growth, adaptability, and security. There will always be more to learn, new configurations to explore, and fresh challenges to tackle. Just like Alex, your adventure with Intune is what you make of it.

www.ingramcontent.com/pod-product-compliance
Lightning Source LLC
LaVergne TN
LVHW022124060326
832903LV00063B/3689